Digital Employee Experience

Put Your Employees First Towards a More Human Digital Workplace

Christiaan Lustig

Tabhita Minten

Digital Employee Experience

Tabhita Minten
Christiaan Lustig

Authors: Tabhita Minten & Christiaan Lustig
Cover design: Christiaan Lustig
Cover photo: Christina Morillo

ISBN: 978-1-4717-7674-8

www.digital-employee-experience.nl

Foreword

The global pandemic has propelled the world of work into new and more digital practices, and in this environment the concept of the digital employee experience (DEX) will be critical to further shaping outcomes in productive (and enjoyable!) ways. This is because DEX tackles the digital component of employee experience by putting the human at the heart of things.

But if digital employee experience is an important idea, it is a new one, at least in its current form. For this reason, we need pioneers to map out the landscape to enable wider engagement and participation of organisations around the globe.

With their new book "Digital employee experience", Tabhita Minten and Christiaan Lustig have proven themselves to be innovators and visionaries, while keeping connected to the realities of how modern firms work. The book contains a core model that puts shape around DEX by focusing on four perspectives: employee, organisation, technology, and physical environment.

By diving deeper into each of these perspectives, this model will be useful for all teams. As they say in the book: "The larger the perspectives overlap, the more likely the deeper layers come into contact with each other and the closer you come to (a good) digital employee experience".

James Robertson
Managing director of Step Two
Founder of the global DEX movement

Content

1 Introduction

The world is changing faster than ever. We experience that almost daily. Everything is becoming digital, and people have to adapt. Both in their private lives — from online shopping and banking to filing your digital tax return — and at work — from the enormous email culture to working remotely and meeting online.

But did things really change that much? Josh Bersin, global thought leader in human resources and HR technology, does not think so. In January 2021 he declared that work has not actually changed at all for the last forty years (about the duration of his career)[1]. Bersin lists:

1. People come to work to express and share their talents with others.
2. People want to be treated fairly.
3. People want to have the opportunity to learn and grow.
4. People want to be recognised for the contribution they make.
5. People want to feel safe in their work environment.

---

[1] https://joshbersin.com/2021/01/work-is-still-work

According to Bersin, this is the core of work[2]. Independent of organisation, discipline, specialism, and role. We believe that it is precisely in these more universal aspects of working that technology, and in particular digital employee experience, helps to make things easier and sometimes even better.

Before you start reading the next chapters of this book, it is important to have a few definitions clear in advance. What do we mean by digital employee experience? How do we define digital workplace and what do we mean by intranet? Of course, we discuss these concepts extensively in this book, but it is helpful if you already have an idea from the first chapter on.

1. By **digital employee experience** we mean "the sum total of digital interactions within the work environment". Digital employee experience thus provides a holistic and strategic view of digital work and collaboration and its impact on people and organisations. We will also use the abbreviation DEX.

2. A **digital workplace** is (a) "a set of tools, platforms and environments for work", and (b) "a great digital workplace consists of a holistic set of tools, platforms and environments for work, delivered in a coherent, usable and productive way".

---

[2] Things that we all already know from Maslow's hierarchy of needs.

3. Finally, a concept that we will also use: an **intranet** is (a) "an internal network that uses the same methodology and techniques as the Internet but is accessible only to employees".[3] And (b) a modern intranet acts as the main digital entrance to information and crucial services for various groups of employees.

Of course, you can endlessly dispute these kinds of definitions. And that happens a lot. We have taken these versions from the work of James Robertson[4], among others. However, the second definition of intranet (at b) is of ourselves.

What can you expect from this book? First and foremost: this is not a handbook that helps you to get started with digital employee experience in concrete terms. As far as we are concerned, this is impossible for two reasons:

1. DEX is still a relatively young concept and there are very few organisations (at least in the Netherlands and Belgium) that have already taken firm steps with this.
2. On top of that, working on digital employee experience is (and should be) extremely intertwined with your organisational context. This includes diversity in employees, functions, culture, leadership style,

---

[3] https://www.gartner.com/en/information-technology/glossary/intranet
[4] https://www.slideshare.net/jamesr/dex-the-way-ahead-keynote-at-intrateam-event-in-copenhagen-march-2020

stakeholders involved, and components of your digital workplace. We believe each organisation should have its own (tailor-made) approach.

That is why in this book we explain the origin of digital employee experience, which perspectives we distinguish in our DEX Model, which stakeholders are relevant, and where we think the concept stands in general.

From chapter 7 we give some perspectives on how we see the application of digital employee experience in organisations. With these, we hope to offer you inspiration on how to get started with digital employee experience yourself, and gain experience in your own organisation.

So, if we are to believe Bersin, work has not necessarily changed. And according to Robertson, the digital workplace is primarily intended to support people's work. We believe that people – whether you call them employees, co-workers or colleagues — should be at the forefront when it comes to digitalisation. And note, we do not say 'put the employee *at the centre*' but 'put the employee *first*'. It is easier for people, teams, and organisations to have their own interests in mind than to put themselves in the shoes of others. When the employee comes first, it becomes clear whose interests should prevail, and who should really empathise with whom.

Just as physical work environments such as offices, shops, restaurants, and factories do not consist of only stone, metal, and glass, so the intranet, digital workplace, and digital employee experience are certainly not just about bits and bytes. It is all about people.

Utrecht, December 2021
Tabhita Minten
Christiaan Lustig

2 *Back to the future*: a workday in 2020

At the beginning of this book, we are going on a journey. A journey through time. Just as Marty McFly went back to 1955 in the film *Back to the Future* (1985) to make sure his parents fall in love. In *Back to the Future part II* (1989), Marty travels from 1985 to the then-distant future, to 2015. But when the villain of the film steals the DeLorean time machine, he must go back to 1955. Marty keeps travelling back and forth between past, present, and future.

We now also travel back to the spring of 2010 and look forward from the then-present day to a knowledge worker's day in the then distant future of 2020. After that (in the next chapters of this book) we also go *back to the future* to see where digital work and collaboration really stands, now that 2021 has almost ended.

Christiaan, our very own Marty McFly, is speaking.

***

SOMETIME IN MAY 2010

For the last few months, I have been coming across the New Way of Working. Apparently, we will all soon be working independent of time and location, and merging our work and private lives. Face-to-face conversations with colleagues, customers, and partners will become less frequent. To see what this New Way of Working may look like, I will give an outline of a workday in mid-2020.

7.00-9.30: read new messages first: everything in one inbox

Get up on time in the morning and shower. I dress the kids and have breakfast with them, and, as soon as they got picked up by the school shuttle bus, I start working, just checking my inbox at home. All data shows up in my personal digital assistant (PDA). We used to have smartphones like the BlackBerry, iPhone 4, and the Samsung Galaxy S, these quasi-PDAs of the early 2000s everyone forgot. I project my messages onto my TV screen.

All online communication via one inbox

E-mail, texts, voicemails, messages from different social media, DMs (direct messages) and the latest news, of course based on my own preferences and interests: I receive everything in the same application. It doesn't matter through which medium the message comes in, and I also don't have to worry about through which medium I answer. My PDA is always online, so I constantly get the messages most important and relevant for me. Posts for work, the sports club, from friends, and updates from my family members may be mixed up, but I can always choose whether I want to see one or more categories.

9.30-12.00: login to co-location and getting started; consultation with colleague

After rush hour, take a bus and train to the office, and go through some messages and reports. I call a colleague who is back from vacation today. Everything with my PDA, while listening to Bach's *Magnificat* with the same device... streaming, of course.

Automatically a workplace at the right location

Now to check where I can sit down to work. I have my own workplace on my regular office workday (I work from home for one day, one day at the office, and I am mainly on the road for the other two days), but today I spend an extra morning at the office. With the booking app on my PDA, I already indicated what I wanted to do this morning; complete a report of my previous project and have a conversation about my progress with my manager. I'm assigned a hot desk on the 6th floor. The same floor where I also have my appointment, because the app automatically retrieved this from my calendar.

Biometric security: fingerprint and face scan

In the office, I sign up by running my finger over the scanner. The door opens, a voice welcomes me and confirms that I should go to the 6th floor. In the hall and the elevator, I see the latest news on screens:

- News images
- Projects our company is working on
- Data on the number of incoming calls
- And all kinds of other work-related information

When I get out of the elevator, I see on the wall opposite the elevator door on which side of the floor workplaces are available. (Of course, I could have used the floor plan with walking route on my PDA, but I work on this floor regularly, so I know the way.)

Wireless connection to network and wireless charging

A green light is lit on one of the office islands. I greet my colleagues and sit down. While we catch up, I take my PDA out of my bag and put it on the desk. The camera in the monitor scans my face, confirming it's me. Now I am automatically logged in on this desk, calls are immediately forwarded — that Skype would become so commonplace again, we did not know ten years ago — and I can also immediately use my personal calendar and address book.

PDA as a direct basis for flexible workplace

My PDA connects wirelessly to the network, charges the battery (also wirelessly), switches on the monitor, and shows a digital keyboard on my physical tabletop; a large part of the desk is also a touchpad, because we haven't used computer mice for a few years now. I can also access all my files immediately: they are physically on servers elsewhere in the office — or elsewhere in the country, I don't even know that — but I can access everything. Of course, the desk automatically adjusts its height to my height and seating position.

Working in the same document at the same time as colleagues

I will finalise the report together with the colleague with whom I worked closely on the recently completed project. We have a direct phone and video connection. She works from home today. And both of us can work in the same document at the same time. I see the changes she is making, and she sees what I am adding to the text. It is easy to add photos and project data from the shared library — after all, all the information is on a central and widely available system. I get a DM message from my programme manager who is curious about the report. I immediately share the file that my colleague and I are working on, and the programme manager also takes a look at our progress.

12.00-15.00: discuss results on the way to project location

Then it's time for my appointment with my manager. I take my PDA from the desk and immediately the screen is locked, and calls are no longer forwarded to this workplace. I already indicated on my calendar that I didn't want to be disturbed for an hour, so when people call me now, they go straight to my voicemail. Should I be absent for more than two hours, I will automatically be logged out of this workplace, and it will become available again for a colleague. (Which means, by the way, that you shouldn't just leave your coat and bag lying around...)

We sit down at a table in the meeting room. We discuss the topics I prepared, but my manager also asks about the status of my report. I open the file on my PDA and have it projected onto the digital tabletop. Together we look at what might still be missing.

Listen to project plan summary on the go

After having had lunch with my manager, I go by car — an electric one from a car-sharing company, of course— to a project site for a meeting with colleagues and partners. On the way there, I listen to *the management summary of the project plan: my PDA connects to the intranet for this, converts the document into voice, and sends the stream to the audio system of the car.*

15.00-18.00: texting and project consultation

When I arrive at the location I sign up at the reception. One of the people I am meeting is half an hour late. I can wait in the hall for a moment, which gives me the opportunity to text my partner that I will be home a little later this afternoon. After all, I don't see the other members of my team that often, and I think the appointment is important enough not to want to curtail it.

Make appointments while you wait

In the meantime, I can read some short messages on my PDA. One of them is a request from one of the programme managers to arrange an appointment. I go to the booking app and indicate at which location, with how many people, and for how long we want to meet. Because all invitees share their calendar via intranet, I get a number of options for a date and time. And the app also suggests having lunch delivered, as a meeting between 11am and 2pm is best. I approve, and the appointment will immediately appear on the calendar. Usually, within an hour or two I have received confirmation from most attendees that they will be attending.

Watch video report and jointly update documents

Then the final attendee for my appointment of that afternoon arrives. We walk to the conference room and the other invitees also start coming into the room one after the other. We start with a short video report of the progress of the project so far. I select the right video on my PDA — the file is also on the central server — and send the video directly to the HD projector in this room. After the video we open the schedule and the project plan. We project both documents on the screen, too. The attendees can also work directly in the source file, via their own PDA and the displays, digital keyboards, and touch pads in the table.

Information widely shared, but with various levels of visibility
Financial information is only visible to me and my colleagues, while confidential purchasing data is only visible to me and our supplier. Together we make some changes to the planning. These are automatically sent to the programme managers involved, so they too can keep track of the progress of the project. Other stakeholders — management, support staff, etc. — of suppliers and other parties also receive an update. This gives all people involved the required overview, and moreover they can all respond to our changes. Those suggestions are visibly incorporated into the source documents, and only await approval (or rejection) by the project manager.

18.00-23.00: PDA is also the private hub for all media
In the evening, after dinner, when the children are in bed, I sit down in an easy chair with my PDA. The New Way of Working has now been fully established, but the 'New Way of Education' is still just from 8 in the morning to 4 in the afternoon; after all, children's biological clocks can be controlled less. I check the latest messages from friends and family, see a tip from my brother for an interesting

documentary, and suggest my partner to watch it together. I put my PDA down, and the film streams directly to the TV. We watch the documentary with a good glass of wine, and afterwards we talk some more.

Then it's bedtime and I read another part of the e-book on my PDA, with some relaxed music in the background on the same device. I don't have to set the alarm clock for the next morning, because my PDA knows what time I have to go to work. So, at 6:15 it signals the blinds to open slowly and produces the sound of birds whistling to wake me up.

BACK TO 2010

Good news: a lot of things are already possible
The good news about this outline of a workday in 2020 is that a lot of things are already more or less a reality. Smartphones and tablets are selling by the millions: think of the iPhone 4 and the first iPad, the BlackBerry, the Samsung Galaxy S and Galaxy Tab, and the new HP Touchpad and HP Veer. The fact that with these devices you are not always and everywhere online is almost unthinkable for many. Collaborating with colleagues in the same files or data at the same time is possible with Google Docs and (the more or less flopped) Google Wave. You listen to music streaming with Spotify, save and edit files from your PC, laptop or smartphone in Dropbox, wireless charging is already possible with the Touchstone from HP (formerly Palm) — my electric toothbrush can even do it — and e-mail, social media and other online means of communication are increasingly

coming together in one place, for example in your Facebook Social Inbox.

Significant impact on the organisation of today
This New way of Working and the steps towards it have significant consequences for how we organise things now. For instance:

- You need to connect different systems such as ERP and CRM-like applications, file servers and (the web-based) intranet.
- Searching across these various systems (meta search) will become crucial, as will identification and classification (metadata) of all this data.
- And what about filtering, access, and security for all employees, but also for your customers and partners.
- This requires much more openness than there often is now, as does flexibility — the expression 'Design for Change' sticks with me in this regard.
- And you can demand responsibility from employees, which of course must be matched by trust.

Shifting functions and tasks from workstation to apps
There is a huge fence around the enormous amount of functionality and data that ERP and CRM systems and intranet tools contain. That is good from a security point of view, but for the people who want (and have to) work like in the outline given, it is an unnecessary boundary. Because these functions and tasks are shifting from desktop PCs and laptops, via browsers on smartphones, tablets, to widgets

and (mobile) apps. These apps unlock more and more (sub) functions of ERP, CRM, and intranet tools: contact (email, SMS, voicemail, messaging), calendar, work descriptions and procedures, relations' data, and project information, and booking facilities. Moreover, many of those apps know where they are: after all, some functions are (much) more important in certain places than others.

Task-oriented focus

The first step to take in all these developments should be a sharp focus on tasks, not from a single system, but across multiple systems. Receive and send messages, make an appointment, find a procedure, declare travel expenses, or find a colleague who can help with a specific problem. Employees want to have the right tools and information available at their fingertips at the right time and not limited by where they are located.

***

And now it is back to the future for us as well, because what is the status of digital work and collaboration now that 2021 has almost ended?

3 What is (digital) employee experience?

Technology now acts as the central nervous system in most organisations. Technological elements play a role in every improvement or innovation. So, the technological environment is a major influence on the cultural and physical environment of employees. Together, these three environments have a major influence on how employees experience their work and how this corresponds to their own needs, expectations and wishes.

You work on a great employee experience by tackling, improving, and innovating things in the three environments of the employee — cultural, technological, and physical — in conjunction with each other. As a result, employees not only come to work because they *need to*, but also really much *want to* work in an organisation. Digital employee experience is an important part of this.

3.1 DEX definition

In February 2018, Robertson wrote his first article about Digital Employee Experience (DEX). This makes him the founder of this concept.

Robertson's definition is this:

*Digital employee experience is the sum total of
the digital interactions within the work environment.*[5]

Robertson purposely defines the DEX concept broadly: "... so that it provides a way to bring together previously uncoordinated digital activities within an organisation".

Digital employee experience provides a framework for organisations to jointly address technological developments and projects with different departments in a more holistic way, from the perspective of employees, and to align them with broader organisational goals. What helps is that it is an innovative concept that seems to be landing in the boardroom as well as in project teams and in different departments, so it really puts developments such as the digital workplace in a broader perspective.

Besides, it is a concept that organisations and employees can further investigate and shape themselves to suit their own context. Finally, digital employee experience offers new ways to understand how organisations can work in remote, digital,

---

[5] https://www.steptwo.com.au/papers/what-is-digital-employee-experience

asynchronous and hybrid ways, and what the impact of these ways of working is on employees (be it positive or negative).

3.2 What is employee experience?

In almost a decade, the customer experience has become the focus of all kinds of organisations. It is no longer just about the products and services that companies provide, but also about the way in which they deliver them. What experiences do customers have at different touchpoints in their customer journey and how can we make those experiences as positive as possible? Now that customer experience has really taken hold, it is becoming increasingly clear that the role of employees is crucial. Because if you take good care of your employees, they take good care of your customers.

Just like customer experience (CX) focuses on the optimal customer experience, employee experience (EX) focuses on the experience of employees. Employee experience is what a (potential) employee experiences in an organisation and how this matches a person's expectations. From the presentation of the organisation and applying for a job to the moment the employee leaves the organisation, and even after that... and everything that happens at work in between.

There are now countless definitions of employee experience, but they often have the same characteristics. We use the definition and models of Jacob Morgan, futurist, and author of

The Employee Experience Advantage as a foundation[6]. Morgan was the first to conduct extensive research at a large number of organisations, and he has also been working on this theme for quite some years. He combines a broad view of all aspects of employee experience with practical tools to get started within different domains in organisations.

Morgan approaches employee experience from two viewpoints:

Figure 1: Employee Experience Design by Jacob Morgan

- For **employees,** their employee experience is simply the reality of what it is like to work in their organisation on a daily basis.

---

[6] Jacob Morgan, *The Employee Experience Advantage: How to Win the War for Talent by Giving Employees the Workspaces they Want, the Tools they Need, and a Culture They Can Celebrate* (New Jersey: John Wiley & Sons Inc, 2017)

- For the **organisation,** the employee experience is what is designed and created for employees, or what the organisation thinks the employees' reality should look like.

The ideal scenario is when the organisation designs or does something and employees perceive it in the intended way. According to Morgan, it is crucial for success that employees actually help shape their experiences themselves instead of simply letting the organisation design them. The employee experience can potentially be 'everything' in an organisation, and therefore be a huge task, but Morgan makes it more tangible by introducing focus in his definition:

Employee experience is designing an organisation
where people want to show up by focusing on
the cultural, technological, and physical environments.

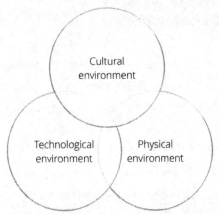

Figure 2: The three environments that affect EX by Jacob Morgan

By formulating employee experience in this way, on the one hand the entire relationship and journey that an employee experiences during their interaction with an organisation is summarised. While on the other hand there is also separation between three different environments: cultural, physical, and technological.

3.3 Working on employee experience

According to Morgan, everything in an organisation now and in the future will fall into just the three environments, which represent the physical space, the culture of the organisation, and technology. From his research Morgan has formulated seventeen attributes that have been incorporated into these acronyms:

- COOL (office spaces)
- CELEBRATED (culture)
- ACE (technology)

The specific attributes are indicators in Morgan's Employee Experience Index. With this index, organisations can test for themselves where they stand in terms of employee experience.

3.3.1 Physical environment: COOL office spaces

The physical environment is everything you can see, touch, taste, and smell. It is the work environment, whether it is an office building, a laboratory, or a factory floor. But also, the characteristics of your colleagues (old, young, male, female, etc.), the art on the wall, and the lunches in the restaurant.

Your physical work environment affects how you feel at work. Do you get energy from it or not? Are you inspired by it? According to Morgan, four attributes are important for a pleasant physical work environment, which together comprise thirty percent of the employee experience.

The C in COOL spaces stands for *Chooses to bring in friends or visitors*. Would an employee bring family and friends to work if the opportunity existed? That certainly gives an indication of how proud employees are of their work environment and how much they feel at home there.

The two O's stand for *Organization's values are reflected* and *Offers flexibility and encourages autonomy* (for example, to determine where and when you work). In terms of values, these are often formulated in intangible words such as trust, collaboration, or openness. The trick is to allow such values to come to life in the physical work environment and thus make them tangible.

Finally, the L stands for *Leverages multiple workspace options*. For example, does the organisation offer open spaces, quiet spaces, project spaces and/or a café setting that match the specific assignment or task you have?

3.3.2 Cultural environment: CELEBRATED culture

The cultural environment is all you feel. It is the vibe you get when you walk in the door through shared values, behaviours, and ways of working within an organisation. Organisational culture exists regardless of whether an organisation takes action on it. It is, like the air, present, without us being constantly aware of it. This contrasts with the physical and technological environment that the organisation must actively design and create. That is why, Morgan says, it is important that organisations design and create their culture and not simply let it exist (or worse, fester).

Morgan distinguishes no fewer than ten attributes for the cultural environment that together comprise forty percent of the employee experience.

- *Company is viewed positively.* A good reputation ensures that employees work for an organisation with pride. They want to feel good about the company they work for and tell others about it.
- *Everyone feels valued.* This variable focuses on recognition and appreciation of employees. People want to feel valued at work. They want their presence and involvement to be

noticed and their ideas listened to. In addition, they want appropriate compensation for the work done.

- *Legitimate sense of purpose.* In successful organisations people work together towards a goal that motivates them. As a result, they feel connected to the organisation and are more likely to do their best because they want to, not just because they have to.
- *Employees feel like they are part of a team.* Work is a team sport, and the best organisations have their employees work together in different teams. This may depend on location or on a specific problem to be solved, requiring a number of different specialties. Dynamic and fluid collaboration goes far beyond the organisational chart. Stimulating and rewarding team performance is also central in such an organisational culture.
- *Believes in diversity and inclusion.* Diverse organisations bring together and blend people from all backgrounds, religions, races, sexual orientations, and generations to work well together. In an inclusive environment, employees are also free to be themselves and share their unique points of view.
- *Referrals come from employees.* If employees are proud of their organisation and feel valued, they will also recommend the organisation to others. Just as they talk privately about a nice film or give a friend a tip for a good restaurant, they may also want to share their workplace with others. And in this way, they can enthuse their former classmates, friends, family, and others in their

network to connect of even work at the organisation as well.

- *Ability to learn new things and given resources to do so and advance.* Development programmes, training and modern technology can encourage employees to learn something new and keep them engaged and moving forward.
- *Treats employees fairly.* Difficult situations can arise at work, but the best organisations treat their employees fairly. That means there are no prejudices about certain ideas or types of people and real commitment is noticed by people who can make a difference.
- *Executives and managers are coaches and mentors.* Gone are the days when management looked down on employees and lead the organisation from the top. Today, leaders are among their employees in the workplace, collaborating, encouraging, and coaching their employees throughout their jobs and careers.
- *Dedicated to employee health and wellness.* Forward-thinking organisations realise that well-being is related to job performance and are offering employees ways to improve their health at work and at home.

3.3.3 Technological environment: ACE technology

Finally, the technological environment refers to the interaction between employees and the systems and tools they use, where the word 'interaction' according to Morgan is crucial. This is a clear similarity with Robertson's definition of DEX.

Morgan says, "Although we view technology as something that lives in a separate, nonhuman bucket, technology has a palpable impact on the organisation — it is what we use to communicate, collaborate, and actually get our jobs done".

The technology environment includes PCs, laptops, and approved smartphones as well as the HR system, intranet, document management system and video conferencing solutions. But also, apps, text processing software, e-learning tools and, the user interface and design elements of systems.

Technology has now become the central nervous system in organisations, which we can no longer do without: "If the tools break down, then everything else around them, including the human relationships, also breaks down". Research has shown that malfunctioning systems can cause enormous frustration and time loss and can also be a major reason for people to eventually quit their jobs.

Morgan distinguishes three attributes here that together comprise the last thirty percent of employee experience.

1. Available to everyone
The first feature seems fairly basic. Make sure that all systems and tools are usable by all employees who want them. It often happens that only certain groups of employees have access to the latest technology. This can cause irritation, frustration and

resentment and thus negatively affect the total employee experience.

If you really want to take a big step forward, according to Morgan, you not only give employees access to as much technology as possible at work, but you also make software available for personal use.

2. Consumer-grade technology

The second attribute refers to tools and systems that are so beautiful, usable, and valuable that employees would consider using them privately.

You see the opposite happening in practice: the organisation offers a robust, secure, and scalable enterprise system; employees find it ugly, cumbersome, and old-fashioned and resort to modern tools that they use in their private lives. So, the trick is to look closely at technology that we use every day in our private lives.

3. Employee needs vs business requirements

Morgan points out that those who formulate requirements for systems in organisations are often different from the people who will use the system. This first group of people makes a complete program of requirements, which can be checked off nicely. They then select a system that meets all requirements and that is also technically sound. But the result? A system that is unworkable in practice. For a good employee experience, tools and systems need to consider how and why employees actually work.

3.4 Focus on DEX

Back to digital employee experience. You can plot this concept one-on-one on the specific technological environment of Morgan's employee experience model, but we think it is more than that. We do find the three characteristics of ACE technology appealing and logical, but we also find them rather thin given the impact that technology and digitalisation have on our lives both professionally and personally.

Technology influences the way we behave. We have almost fused with our smartphones, our children are digital natives, our homes and offices are becoming smarter, and we are discussing who will be responsible for the actions of our self-driving cars.

Most organisations undergo a continuous digital transformation, and technological components play a role in every improvement or innovation, including in the physical and cultural environment. Consider, for example, the application of sensors in office environments, where Morgan's physical and technological environment will intertwine. We will certainly go into more detail on this in Chapter 4.

Technology also offers new opportunities for organisations that we cannot even imagine in advance, for example the emergence of all kinds of new business models. This goes further than making the right, attractive technical systems available to the right people in line with the way they work. In the meantime, we mainly hear from employees: "No, not another new system. We already have so many".

We agree with the advice regarding employee needs versus business requirements. But while Morgan seems to focus on collaboration between HR (Human Resources) and IT (Information Technology) and improving HR systems, we take the entire digital workplace, including all kinds of business and support systems, as our starting point.

Employees have increasingly higher expectations of their work environment. Meeting those higher expectations and offering a great (digital) employee experience means that organisations are becoming more complex. To cope with this complexity, people have to work together even more.

Therefore, organisations really need to work on a digital workplace that actually supports people in their daily work and collaboration with others. This also means that many more departments should work together, and that knowledge of, for example, information technology is no longer the sole preserve of the IT department.

The attributes Morgan mentions, are rather ordered by domain. The danger of this division is that everyone will work on their own piece of the puzzle, in their own department, while (digital) employee experience is pre-eminently about the coherence of things.

3.4.1 DEX and 'digital' culture

Digitalisation requires different, new skills that not everyone may easily acquire. There is an interaction between the needs of employees and the direction of the organisation. We see that new features and tools are introduced into organisations every week (think of recent systems and platforms, such as Slack, Office 365, etc.), but this is of little benefit if employees do not have sufficient skills to communicate and collaborate digitally, even though they may want to.

Additionally, digital transformation requires a "digital" culture that enables an organisation to adapt quickly and fundamentally to new circumstances. So, there is a direct link with the cultural environment of Morgan. How do you ensure that employees, the organisation, and technology are in balance? In chapters 7, 8 and 9 we provide some examples and suggestions on how you can deal with this as an organisation.

3.4.2 Work smart together

Swedish digital strategist Oscar Berg speaks of a 'big picture' approach[7]; to create a truly valuable digital workplace and digital employee experience, the technological, physical, and cultural environments must be developed in conjunction with each other under the motto 'work smarter together'. The more cohesion, the happier and more productive employees will be.

According to Berg, a critical condition in the rapidly changing environment in which organisations find themselves is effective leadership. He offers three pieces of advice:

1. Create a specific, clear, and connecting vision.
2. Put people at the forefront of all your developments (adopt a *people-first* mindset).
3. Work from a learning process.

With the third advice, Berg refers to a holistic, iterative, and employee-oriented approach based on Design Thinking. This fits in well with the strategic, but at the same time pragmatic approach to digital employee experience in organisations, which we also use in practice.

In the next chapter we will explain this 'big-picture' approach using our own model. In chapter 5 we will then show how we

---

[7] That is what he did on the Brussels Intranet & Digital Workplace Conference on 23 May 2019.

further develop the principle of 'work smart together' in the model.

4 Four perspectives on digital employee experience

In our daily practice over the past years, parallel to the work that Morgan, Robertson and also Jane McConnell did, we have been working on our own DEX Model. In our view, to work on digital employee experience in an in-depth way, you need to look at the challenges from at least four perspectives.

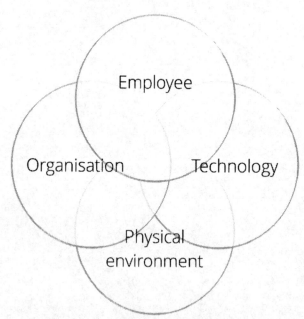

Figure 3: The four perspectives on DEX

- **The perspective of the employee** is about how your colleagues do their work: what are they facing? Which tools do they use for their daily work, and how pleased or disgruntled are they with them? What is the influence of processes and procedures on their work? Which level of digital skills do employees have?

- **The perspective of the organisation** is about which ambitions and goals, and which strategy they have mapped out. What opportunities and threats are there? In which of those do digital developments play a role? What is your culture like, and what is the impact of leadership style?

- **The perspective of the technology** is, of course, about applications and systems, but also about your organisation's vision for them. How do you see the support of day-to-day work by tools? What does this mean for the application landscape? How do you view the digital workplace and how does one applications affect the other?

- **The perspective of the physical environment** is about the impact of the physical workplace on digital work and collaboration: which roles and functions are there in your organisation, and where do these people do their work? Is that mainly in the office, or on the road, in workshops or in warehouses? How often do people work from home? This perspective also concerns the ever-increasing digitalisation in the physical environment. What does this mean for your organisation and digital employee experience?

We will discuss each of these perspectives in more detail in this chapter. We start with the perspective that we find is the most important, namely that of the employee.

4.1 Employee perspective

The first perspective that we want to address is the employee perspective. Starting with the employee is the foundation of our model, and the employee is the substance of digital employee experience in a broader sense. The employee comes first in our DEX Model. This means that their needs and expectations of employees are at the forefront.

Behaviour
Goal
Needs

Employee

Figure 4: The three layers of the employee's perspective

Three factors are important when it comes to the employee's perspective. Three layers that you can distinguish, when it comes to your colleagues. Looking from the outside in, you will see:

- First of all, people's **behaviour**, both in a physical and in a digital environment.
- Beneath this, there is a **goal** a person wants to achieve, a task that someone wants to perform to get work done.
- And underneath that lie the **needs** that are behind people's motivation, purpose, and behaviour.

4.1.1 Making choices based on empathy and evidence

To gain a good understanding of what employees want and (especially!) what they need in their daily work, on one hand it is good to gain real empathy for employees and their needs. On the other hand, you need evidence from observing their behaviour in a digital workplace. Too much focus on empathy does not make things tangible enough, while too much focus on evidence causes the human aspects to disappear. The combination of the two provides what is needed for this part of DEX.

Evidence

In the field of customer experience, it has long been common practice to put the customer first. Customer experience platforms continuously monitor customer activity to provide them with the right information or products at the right time. Data analysis plays a crucial role, here. The term 'big data' seems to be out of fashion nowadays, but is the core: the more data from customers you have, the better you can 'predict' what to do for them and when.

We are very much in favour of observation: which behaviour does your employee display in which situation? Behaviour is related to the technology that the employee uses. This might be your intranet, or your personnel administration or logistics system, or any digital platform for that matter. You can analyse behaviour from usage data, or (usability) tests. This is valuable in and of itself… but statistics of your systems or digital workplace as a whole, also have two major disadvantages:

a. They only measure what you currently offer.
b. They are influenced by how good (or bad) this is currently being found.

Relying solely on usage statistics to align your digital workplace more closely with the needs and expectations of employees is one of the pitfalls we often encounter. But it is the first, outer layer of the employee's perspective: behaviour on digital platforms.

Empathy
Not a single organisation will say that it does not put its employees first, whether it is a commercial enterprise, non-profit organisation, or government agency. But in all these organisations it emerges time and again this is easier said than done. This is quite understandable because as human beings

we are unconsciously focused on our own group. And if you read 'department' for 'group', you probably immediately understand where the problem lies.

We are programmed as human beings to improve the conditions for our own group. And for many people, colleagues are not part of this group. In our daily work we often see that many companies and institutions take the organisational perspective as the starting point for the employee- or demand-based design of internal digital communication, services, and collaboration. As a result, those resources and processes are not really (or really not!) employee- or demand-based.

So, how do you find out what your employee needs from you? This can be done, for example, with one-on-one interviews or group discussions/focus groups. From these discussions, you retrieve how people do their work, how they experience it, how they find information, and which tools and systems they use. But also, which (digital) skills they have. This provides you with valuable insights.

This concerns the second or middle layer of the employee's perspective: which goals does your employee have, what task do they want (or have to) perform? You cannot understand this from just your data. We use a method for this, that reveals which four, five or six items, topics or tasks are most important to employees. And which similarities and differences there may be between groups of employees. This is called task identification.

Underneath those two layers (i.e., behaviour and goal) there is a core: the impetus of your colleagues and their deeper needs. You cannot extract this from data either. You cannot find out with a questionnaire. To get to know the motivation and needs of employees, you will have to talk to them. And that is what many organisations find quite difficult.

Fortunately, your colleague is only human. And most people do not mind talking about themselves at all. On the contrary. So just ask your colleague a few questions. But do not ask questions like: what would you like to find in our digital workplace? Or which new functionality do you find important in that system? That is the wrong focus.

Our experience is that it is very enlightening to simply have a conversation. In interviews or focus groups, we often ask people questions about their personal (home) situation, their background, their education. About their teams and departments, what they must deal with, and how they perceive any work issues. We also ask whether they are usually well helped or not. And what that does to them, how they experience it.

4.1.2 Personas and employee journeys

By now it will be clear to you that you must collect evidence of employee behaviour on digital platforms. And you have to develop an understanding of, and empathy for employees' work context. But when you have collected all those insights, all that data, what do you do with it? This is where personas and employee journeys come into play.

Personas

Personas first: These are fictional, archetypical representations of a group of employees. A persona summarises traits of that group in one fictional character. For example, nurses: they work in a certain way, have certain needs for and expectations of digital work and collaboration, and must be able to do certain things in order to do their job well. You can capture those things in a persona.

But that is not all. To really turn such a fictional employee into a character or persona, you also give them a name, a photo, an educational background, and a home situation. This way your persona really comes to life. Preferably you create a persona together with the group of employees who should actually be represented by said persona.

Why are personas important? Because, through personas, stakeholders, and those involved with the digital employee experience, can identify with a group of employees. They can (better) empathise with the needs of the group which the persona represents and will therefore also more easily make the right choices regarding digital employee experience.

In our experience, a unique addition to personas is the most important questions, tasks, and topics that come from a target group survey. And we mean quantified, because such insights can be obtained through top tasks identification. And with that you add a valuable quantitative part to an otherwise qualitatively founded persona.

Employee journeys
Then there are employee journeys. We look at this in two ways:

- On the one hand, the entire employee journey as the 'journey' that an employee makes through your organisation, so from application through onboarding and promotion to leaving.
- On the other hand, we also divide that overarching journey into parts, and then we also call each of those parts 'employee journeys.

Regarding the second, narrower definition of the employee journey, it is interesting to start from the needs of the employees. Task analysis comes into play here again: which things do employees find most important and what is their experience now? It is again wise to sit down with the target group to map out their own journey together with them. What is relevant here:

- What steps do employees take? What actions do they take? Which tasks do they perform?
- Which tools or systems do they use?
- Which colleagues (or roles) are involved?
- What do employees think about this? How do they experience those steps, tools, and collaboration? What emotions do they have about this?
- What goal(s) do employees want to achieve? What is their motivation? What (deeper) need(s) are they trying to fulfil?

You also plot these different steps and associated experiences together with employees in a journey map. This gives you a good insight into good insight into what happens, why it happens, what sometimes goes wrong, and where — according to employees themselves! — something really needs to be done to make their journey better.

We advocate linking personas and journey maps. You know which groups of employees exist from your target audience research. You make personas from that. You also know what those colleagues find important. You put this into the personas, and it immediately provides you with a starting point for the journey maps. In short: a persona has one or more employee journeys, and each journey belongs to one or more personas.

4.2 The perspective of the organisation

The second perspective is that of the organisation. For the layers, we start from the terms that are used in the various management models and that are particularly relevant when designing a good digital employee experience.

Figure 5: The three layers of the organisational perspective

- **Mission & vision**: Why do you exist as an organisation? What are the ambitions for the future? Which trends and developments are important? Where possible, you can already make a connection here with (digital) employee experience. In chapters 7 to 9 we offer a number of concrete starting points for this.
- **Core values**: What are the norms, values, and beliefs in your organisation? What effect does this have on (digital)

culture and leadership? We will discuss digital culture in detail in chapter 8.

- **Strategy**: What are the short- and long-term targets? How do you want to achieve results, with what approach? The DEX strategy should align with this.

4.3 Tension between wishes and design

A major area of tension in the organisational perspective is what employees expect and how the organisation aligns with this and vice versa, as already visualised in Morgan's employee experience design in Chapter 3.

For optimal (digital) communication, services, knowledge sharing and collaboration between employees, the direction and design of the organisation must be clear. Then you can work from and on common organisational goals. But if the balance tilts too much towards the organisational perspective, employees often seem unable to make their own choices and have to adapt to technical systems and their digital workplace.

The organisational form and structure are also increasingly relevant in this regard. Organisations are increasingly moving from a traditional, hierarchical structure in which employees are told what to do, to new forms of organisation in which trust is the starting point. This gives the employee the right preconditions to make decisions in line with the goals of the organisation.

4.4   The perspective of technology

Third, we (only) discuss the perspective where most questions about digital employee experience seem to start, namely the perspective of technology. In principle, we consider this to be subordinate to the first two. Of course, technology is important — in fact, without technology there would be no digital employee experience at all — but the choices in this area must be fed by the other perspectives.

4.4.1   Jumble of applications and systems

As far back as 2017, Dion Hinchcliffe wrote that key performance indicators from productivity and efficiency to engagement and retention are all influenced by the nature and quality of the digital tools employees receive. He added that the number of devices and applications that employees (must) use to do their work is higher than ever.[8]

As for Hinchcliffe, it is also our experience that in medium and large organisations employees use more than two devices — in addition to desktop or laptop as well as smartphone and/or tablet — and quickly thirty or more applications and systems.

4.4.2   Fragmentation of information

Fragmentation across different systems and devices makes it more difficult to find people and information. Often people do

---

[8] https://www.zdnet.com/article/can-we-achieve-a-better-more-effective-digital-workplace

not know what to do where and moreover, they regularly have different applications to do the same things.

In the technology perspective, it is therefore mainly about identifying the way(s) in which you best support diverse groups of employees with which (combination of) systems and therefore bring cohesion to them. In short, you work on the best suitable digital workplace for your employees and organisation.

As with the previous two perspectives, you can also recognise different layers in the technology perspective. We briefly name the layers here. In chapter 6, we discuss the role of technology within DEX in detail.

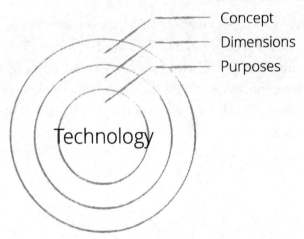

Figure 6: The three layers of the technology perspective

- **Purposes**: The digital workplace is not one thing or application but breaks down into several separate systems and information sources. And within the purpose of the digital workplace, those separate tools each have their own goal or goals.
- **Dimensions**: We distinguish two dimensions in digital work and collaboration using a digital workplace: (a) type of work and (b) frequency of use.
- **Concept**: The digital workplace flourishes due to a certain degree of cohesion between different systems. This (design) concept largely depends on purpose(s) and dimensions.

4.5   The perspective of the physical environment

Jacob Morgan also mentions the fourth perspective of the physical work environment. This concerns the place where people do their work, what this environment radiates and where the connection is with the digital employee experience. Again, there are different layers to distinguish within this perspective.

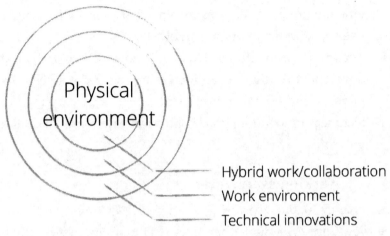

Hybrid work/collaboration

Work environment

Technical innovations

Figure 7: The three layers of perspective of the physical environment

From the inside out:

- **Hybrid work/collaboration**: Working remotely (and or work from home, which is not the same) — for example one day a week — has become increasingly common in recent years, but COVID-19 has of course accelerated this enormously. In addition, a new challenge has arisen, because some employees will continue to work remotely and/or more often, while others will still prefer the office environment. This has an enormous impact on DEX in the coming years and thus forms the inner circle of this perspective.
- **Work environment:** Your physical work environment and the way you do your work in it has a major influence on your digital needs and therefore forms the second layer within this perspective. It makes a substantial difference

whether, for example, you are almost always on the road or usually work in an open-plan office.

- **Technical innovations**: Due to social and technological developments, there is an increasing overlap between the physical and digital environment, which is why we refer to technical innovations in the physical environment as the outermost layer.

4.5.1 Working everywhere

According to the NWCS (Netherlands Working Conditions Survey)[9], in 2019 more than 1 in 3 Dutch employees (37%) sometimes worked from home, of which 2% usually. On average, employees worked 6.1 hours a week from home. Sector differences were large: in the hospitality industry (10%), agriculture (17%), and transport (21%) the fewest people work from home, while working from home in financial services (73%), ICT (72%), and education (68%) was common.

As a result of the COVID-19 pandemic and the accompanying measures, working from home increased significantly in 2020. Almost half (47%) of employees sometimes worked from home: 15% usually worked from home and 32% combined working from home with working on location. On average, employees worked 19.4 hours a week from home. There were also major differences between sectors in 2020. Commerce

---

[9] NCWS information, data and publications are available on: https://www.monitorarbeid.tno.nl/en-us/surveys/nwcs/

(26%), agriculture (18%) and catering (12%) were the least likely to work from home. Financial services (91%), ICT (89%) and business services (61%) were the most likely to work from home.

Teleworking (at least half a day a week outside the company location with access to the company's ICT system) also increased in 2020 (31 % compared to 18% in 2019).

We wonder to what extent this trend will continue in the coming years. Almost 1 in 4 Dutch employees that worked from home in 2020 indicated that they also want to work largely from home after the COVID-19 pandemic. In addition, 43% want to combine working from home with working on location. On average, people want to work from home for 18 hours. The nature of the work, less travel time and better productivity are important reasons for wanting to work (partly) from home in the future. It is striking that the work-life balance is about as often a reason to work on location as to want to work at home.

Several (international) companies are making the complete transition to remote working, but in the Netherlands, we expect a large number of organisations to be more committed to a combination with hybrid working, in line with the wishes of employees. You can read more about this in chapter 7.

4.5.2 Not just open-plan offices

In many ideal scenarios, everyone works in a spacious, green, bright open-plan office — they have their own problems, by the way — but we work for all kinds of organisations that have very diverse workplaces. For example:

- (Higher) education and universities with lecturers in the classroom, researchers in the lab, student psychologists on campus.
- Hospitals and care institutions with nurses at the bedside, surgeons in ORs, doctors on their rounds, the pharmacist in the, er... pharmacy.
- Municipalities and other governmental organisations with people in social district teams, in public gardens, et cetera who do not always have their own fixed workplace.
- Holiday parks with employees in shops, restaurants and swimming pools, and often also part-time and holiday workers.
- Technical organisations with thousands of technicians who use specialist screens and other equipment and maintenance technicians who work for instance in people's homes.
- Production companies with employees on the assembly line and distribution centres with order pickers.

DEX is therefore not only about 'the average employee' — many organisations think of the knowledge worker behind the desk — but also about people without a desk, without a fixed

PC and without a large screen. We should also support them in their daily work, in their own context.

4.5.3 Technical innovations

Social and technological developments are blurring the distinction between the physical and digital environment. The environments must increasingly be designed in conjunction with each other, so that they complement each other optimally.

Virtually close through real-life experiences

Technology can ensure that we also experience virtual real proximity to locations and other people. This makes it seem like we are in the same place as colleagues, even if they are at home, at a different work location or, for example, in another country.

Think of augmented reality (AR) — where information is projected onto the physical environment — for example in the maintenance of aircraft, machinery, or medical equipment.
But think also of, sensors in both devices and buildings, so that you can access a workspace, meeting room or server room with your smartwatch, for example. And even more advanced, that all necessary facilities, including the right light, are ready for you when you walk into a meeting room.

... and virtual reality (VR)

In terms of virtual reality (VR) — where you are completely immersed in a virtual 3D world — we see opportunities to facilitate the same group of employees without a fixed desk and fixed PC (which we mentioned earlier) in their own context. For example, to be able to participate virtually in consultations at the office, where virtual reality can provide a sense of (digital) proximity and people therefore really feel that they are working together. Finally, virtual reality can also offer all kinds of new possibilities for the informal connection between people. In chapter 9 we will give a glimpse into how this can already work in practice.

And from digital twin...
The latest important developments to mention here for the physical work environment and DEX are the *Internet of Things* (objects connected to the Internet), digital *twins* and artificial intelligence.

A digital twin or digital twin is a digital copy of a physical object, such as a lamppost. The digital variant exactly mimics the physical behaviour of the product. For this, all data of the object is collected in one specific place on a server or in the cloud. Suppose you want to know whether you need to carry out maintenance on the lamppost. Then you could read all individual sensors and analyse yourself whether maintenance is necessary, but that takes a lot of time and energy. It is much easier to ask the digital twin, which collects all the data and acts on it.

For example, Rijkswaterstaat (part of the Dutch Ministry of Infrastructure and Water Management) has turned the new tunnel that connects motorways A16 and A13 in Rotterdam-North into a digital twin. This Twin-16 helps to see whether the real road outside is being built according to the requirements that have been set in advance. The concept of digital twins does not only apply to objects and products, but can also be applied to infrastructure, offices, factories and even cities.

... to avatar
With the help of digital twins, it is easier to access data from things connected to the internet and we are also more able to get (new) insights.

One step further is if the digital twins themselves start to observe, reason, and manifest themselves independently. This is possible thanks to the advance of machine learning and other forms of artificial intelligence. Then we start moving towards the (digital) avatar, that we also know from the gaming world (or from the cinema).

"Avatar" refers to a (virtual) entity that can impersonate a human or object. The digital avatar can act independently on behalf of the person in the real world. If you connect various avatars, they can also work together, divide tasks more efficiently, improve processes, run simulations, and make consequences understandable for people. This offers enormous possibilities in all kinds of aspects of the work environment.

Each employee an avatar?

You can also use an avatar as a modern variant of the personal assistant. You can share information with other avatars (and therefore people) via your personal avatar. But you can also let your avatar perform certain things autonomously, such as making appointments, placing orders, or signing contracts. These interactions take place in the virtual world. Your personal avatar functions as the bridge to this world. In this way, people and machines will soon be able to work closely together and they may become each other's colleagues.

4.6 Ambition for DEX: Increase overlap

In the previous paragraphs, we have described the four perspectives and the three layers per perspective. If we include all the layers of the DEX Model, the complete model is created (see next page).

As you can see in the model, the four perspectives partly overlap. The more the perspectives overlap, the greater the chance that the deeper layers come into contact with each other and the closer you come to (a great) digital employee experience.

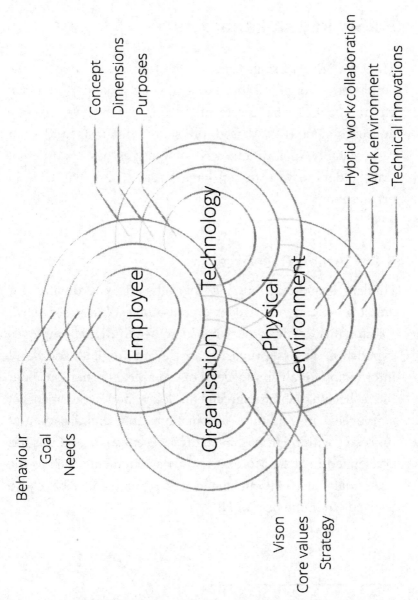

Figure 8: DEX Model with all layers in the four perspectives

5 Six key stakeholders

The DEX Model brings together the four perspectives of the employee, organisation, technology, and physical environment. To be successful in this, we believe that the approach should be based on shared interests and joint responsibility. In addition, we distinguish at least six different stakeholders[10] , who (must) have a seat at the DEX table in organisations.

5.1 Human Resources

Human Resources (HR) is logically the coordinator for employee experience in many organisations. We also see a clear role for this department, when it comes to digital employee experience. HR is primarily a relevant (digital) source of information for all employees. For example, information about the collective labour agreement, leave and assessment of employees. In addition, automation, and digitalisation of processes within HR has taken off in recent years and this has accelerated in 2020. More recently, developments such as the use of data, artificial intelligence and virtual reality have also been added in the field of HR.

---

[10] In this case, we use the term stakeholders for roles, teams, departments, services, etc.

Slightly less eye-catching, but also relevant, is the role of HR when it comes to (digital) culture and digital skills. Digitalisation is leading to fundamental changes. Not only in the competences and skills that are necessary to be able to continue doing the work, but also in the way in which we (digitally) communicate, collaborate, and learn. In addition to technical skills, this requires soft skills, such as empathy, creativity, critical thinking, and change readiness.

Finally, themes such as happiness at work, well-being and involvement of employees, a good work-life balance and greater flexibility in the labour market have received even more attention than before under the influence of COVID-19. For years in a row there has been an increase in workload, stress and burnouts and also reduced involvement. The current crisis affects this in many ways. A key role in this is played by the manager. Managers need to have all kinds of new competencies and skills to be able to lead both remotely and in a hybrid situation, in which people blend working from various locations.

One of the first topics that many organisations tackle in the context of (digital) employee experience is the start of new employees in the organisation (onboarding). But also, reboarding, and cross boarding in the event of change of function, major organisational changes, a new way of working or a merger or takeover can be good topics to get started with.

In principle, every phase of the (major) employee journey can serve as a starting point. HR obviously plays a key role in this.

5.2 Communication

In the internal digital domain, Communication has traditionally been concerned with news (editorial) and the reference or library function on, for example, intranet. Traditionally, this was rather one-sided from the organisation to employees. Under the influence of, among other things, the rise of social media, this now increasingly involves dialogue.

Internal social networks and social intranet facilitate interaction between organisation and employees as well as between employees themselves. As a result, Communication has increasingly taken on a role when it comes to connection, engagement, knowledge sharing and collaboration and facilitating this in, for example, internal communities. This role has only expanded due to COVID-19. Moreover, (online) listening is more important than ever. Because employees work at different places and times, there is less informal meeting between employees, and management is also less aware of what is going on.

For digital employee experience we see a connecting role for Communication. Communications consultants have (if all is well) the expertise and experience to think about all kinds of topics with the target groups in mind. This often makes them the feelers and connectors in organisations. They can bring together the various stakeholders and act as playmakers between different disciplines.

The intranet manager (or a similar function) is often already used to working substantively at the intersection of different domains (in any case Communication and IT). In the context of digital employee experience, we see this role develop further into, for example, product owner for DEX.

5.3 Information Technology

Information Technology (IT) obviously has a role when it comes to digital employee experience. First, there is a logical connection because of the technological component. Think of all systems in an organisation, but also hardware, telephones, cabling, Wi-Fi, medical equipment, et cetera. You often see that IT is the first to pick up new developments and innovations in this area.

Secondly, IT is often also an important source of information for employees for information about products and services, software updates and system maintenance. Or think of guidance in the use of systems with training and manuals, requests for more storage space, data management and reporting malfunctions of applications. All aspects of services provided by this department.

Finally, architects, information managers and other IT professionals have been advocating for years for the integration of digital developments into business strategy, more ownership of IT in the business and better alignment with the needs of employees. DEX offers IT a framework to connect all these kinds of cases and projects with a holistic view and to do this in good collaboration with the other stakeholders.

5.4 Facilities Management

The role of Facilities Management (FM) can also develop increasingly under the influence of (digital) employee experience. This does depend on the positioning of FM in an organisation. At present, it is often presented as an executive club, while it is becoming increasingly clear that the environment in which people work has an enormous influence on their experience, perception, and well-being.

Traditionally, the facilities domain has also been an important source of information and for reporting issues: there is a water or light failure, your desk chair is broken, or a department is being redesigned. All forms of information provision and digital services that have a daily impact on the work of employees and often really belong to the basic conditions for a pleasant work environment.

In chapter 4 we have already discussed various technical innovations that affect the physical work environment and that increasingly blur the distinction between physical and digital environments. In 2020, due to COVID-19 and remote working, office use and the entire facilities domain have completely turned upside down. The question is where these developments will lead in the coming years. Do we still have to build and furnish offices? Is the office changing from a daily workplace into a more flexible meeting place? In short, enough to do for Facilities management, especially in combination with the other DEX stakeholders.

5.5   Disciplines meet in the DEX Model

In chapter 4 we described our DEX Model with the four perspectives. You can roughly plot the four stakeholders — HR, Communication, IT and Facilities — on those perspectives:

- The perspective of employees includes your HR department; typically, also the department where employee experience finds fertile ground.
- The perspective technology clearly belongs to the IT department.
- The physical environment perspective fits the responsibility of Facilities Management.
- And that leaves the perspective of the organisation for the Communication department.

Figure 9: The position of the different disciplines in relation to the perspectives on digital employee experience

We already mentioned we are plotting the stakeholders 'roughly', because you might think this is a bit simplistic… and it is. Communication does not only work from an organisational perspective, and HR is not just there for the employee. And as we saw earlier, the activities of IT and Facilities Management are increasingly intertwining.

As far as we are concerned, the crux of the model is in the centre: all four perspectives and all four stakeholders come together in the core of the model, and they all touch on all other aspects as well. At the core of the model, and therefore in the core of thinking about and working on digital employee experience, there is also a shared interest and a joint responsibility. None of the teams or departments can set the direction and bear responsibility alone; they all need each other to support employees as best as possible in their daily work.

5.6 Primary process

HR, Communication, IT and Facility Services are support services or departments. All four are important and all four are necessary, certainly also for digital employee experience, but whatever type of organisation, the more visible work does not happen in these four departments.

Customers, citizens, patients, students, tenants, donors, or guests usually deal with one or more other departments. Which exactly differs per type of organisation and by industry. Together, these teams or services form the primary process, also known as 'the business'. For example, think of:

- Nurses and physicians in healthcare.
- Teachers and researchers in education.
- Sales and marketing people in commercial organisations.
- Maintenance technicians in technical enterprises.

These groups all have their own needs. If you support them in the work they do on behalf of the organisation, they can in turn provide customers, patients, students, citizens, clients and, guests with good products and services.

Because they themselves know best what their working day looks like and what challenges they face, you must involve these colleagues as much as possible from the start in the design, development, implementation, and optimisation of working methods and systems.

5.7 Management

Finally, management is of course a stakeholder when it comes to digital employee experience. Without a sponsor on the board or support from the board, you can start with DEX, but to really get going you need management. Digital employee experience is ultimately something that you must tackle organisation-wide and must be given a clear place in your organisational strategy.

Our experience is that many of the bottlenecks in organisations arise because tasks are passed on from department to department, or fall between departments. And in the end no one really helps the individual employees with what they need. To be able to change this, mission as well as vision, culture, strategy, leadership and capacity are needed.

5.8 DEX Stakeholder Map

This completes the six stakeholders for DEX: HR, Communication, IT and Facilities Management, (the) business department(s), and management or the board of directors. And we conveniently list them together in the DEX Stakeholder Map:

Figure 10: DEX Stakeholder Map with the six stakeholders; also, the 'business' and management play a decisive role

Is management the 'Commander-in-Chief' in this context? Yes... But also no. If management is not necessarily in charge when it comes to digital employee experience, then who is? In our experience, HR, Communication, IT, Facility Management, business, and management have shared interests and a shared responsibility to support employees in such a way that *they* can serve their customers, students, patients, and guests more easily and faster.

For the ownership of an intranet or wider digital workplace, we often recommend an 'Association of Owners'. This is a good and very practical solution that in our opinion also translates very well into an association of owners for digital employee experience.

To prevent a tie in the votes in such an association, the association must choose someone who can make decisions if necessary. That could very well be (higher) management, but that is not necessarily required. The most important thing is that the stakeholders involved put the interests of the employee first and work together.

6 The digital workplace

We cannot talk about digital employee experience in this book without also paying attention to the digital workplace and, more specifically, the intranet as part of it. Intranet has been our expertise for about twenty years and from there we found the broader digital workplace on our path, on the way to the full story of digital employee experience.

In practice, we increasingly come across organisations that are looking for the ideal mix of systems, the ultimate digital workplace. With the rise of Microsoft 365, a new challenge has arisen. That is why you will find a more extensive chapter here about intranet and the digital workplace in relation to (the technology perspective of) digital employee experience.

6.1 You already have a digital workplace

When you use Outlook and Word in an organisation, for example, you already have a digital workplace. Therefore, you also have a digital employee experience. (Whether it is positive or negative, let us say for now.) You probably have more than those two applications, but this is where it starts. Multiple tools, applications, systems, and information sources together form your digital workplace. One of those tools can be your intranet. You could see the digital workplace as shown in the next figure:

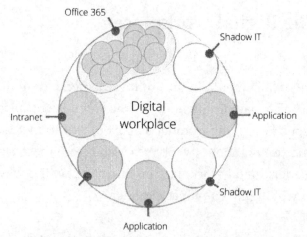

Figure 11: Schematic representation of the digital workplace containing various applications and systems

- **Grey spheres**: different applications and systems together make the digital workplace. Think, for example, of the intranet, the HR system or a DMS (document management system).

- **White spheres**: if you do not offer what employees need (or well), they will automatically find shortcuts. That is where shadow IT comes in: people are looking for their own tools and solutions to still be able to do their work. Often everything they use in their private lives. But personal tools do not always comply with laws that you as an organisation have to comply with, and are often not set up for large-scale and long-term use. In addition, everyone makes their own choice, which means that a joint approach, storage, and agreements are missing. This generally does not benefit your business operations.

- **Light grey underlay with grey spheres**: finally, we have Microsoft 365 which features a prominent place in a growing number of organisations. This is not surprising given the interconnectedness with all kinds of components of office automation for many years (Word, Excel, and PowerPoint), but it does bring its own challenges. We will pay more attention to this later in this chapter.[11]

Fragmentation of information

We already described in chapter 4 that the far-reaching fragmentation across different systems and devices only makes it more difficult to find people and information. The technological environment in which people work is becoming increasingly complex with ever-growing systems, apps, bots and so on. The more systems, the more employees have to figure out and choose what to use for what.

The features in different systems regularly overlap. The fragmentation and continuous growth of new systems also means that it is unclear where the main digital entrance is. Then, as an employee you quickly no longer see the wood for the trees. As you may have already read in the introduction, we see the evolving intranet as the main entrance to the broader digital workplace. This digital entrance, 'front door' or

---

[11] We know that there are also organisations that use Google Workspace, but we hardly come across them in our practice.

'gateway' allows employees to access the apps and tools they most frequently use from one convenient entry point.

6.2 Purpose, dimensions, and design

In chapter 4 we introduced the three layers within the technology perspective: Purposes, Dimensions and Concept. With this we indicate the various ways in which you can best support different groups of employees with which (combination of) systems and thus create cohesion.

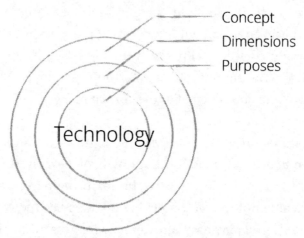

Figure 12: The three layers of the technology perspective

6.2.1 Five purposes

The innermost layer of the technology perspective focuses on the purposes of your modern intranet or digital workplace, which are preferably naturally derived from the organisational objectives. Based on Robertson's Five Purposes[12], we distinguish:

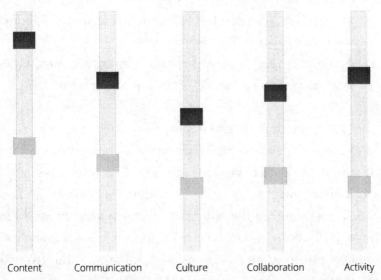

Content   Communication   Culture   Collaboration   Activity

Figure 13: Five purposes of modern intranets by Robertson

1. **Content**: employees can easily find coherent and accessible information in a digital library.
2. **Communication**: the strategic goals are translated to daily work, for example with the help of organisation-wide news, announcements, or weblogs from management, but also, for example, with the help of storytelling and video.
3. **Culture**: the intranet or digital workplace is also a carrier of culture and serves as a means for connection and

---

[12] https://www.Steptwo.com.au/papers/cmb-five-technology/

community building and can therefore also support cultural change.

4. **Collaboration**: groups of employees (teams, departments, projects, etc.) can meet, share knowledge, and collaborate, sometimes also with external partners.

5. **Activity**: employees are supported employees in their daily work to perform all kinds of tasks in different systems.

The interpretation of these purposes and thus the digital workplace depends entirely on your own organisation and organisational objectives. In addition, it is not necessary to work on all purposes at once. The advice is actually not to do this. Depending on the situation in which your organisation finds itself, it can be particularly important to work intensively on one purpose, and perhaps also for a specific group of employees.

By sliding the five purposes like an equaliser you can map the current and the desired situation. Thereafter, the desired situation can be a focus on the short, medium, or long term. This model can therefore be a useful way to map out shared ambitions together with the various stakeholders from chapter 5 and then work on them together.

6.2.2 Two dimensions

The middle layer of the technology perspective focuses on the two dimensions of work and collaboration in a digital workplace, namely type of work and frequency of use.

Dimension: type of work

For the type of work dimension, we first introduce a model based on a 2018 article[13] by Brad Grissom (Digital Transformation Strategist at Microsoft). The article provides an overview of which application from the Microsoft 365-line best suits which type of work (communication, collaboration, concentrated individual work).

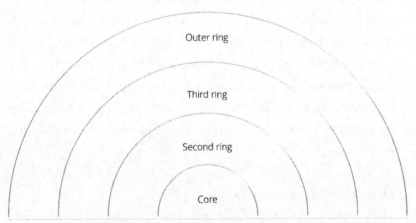

Figure 14: Where work gets done. Or… what to use when? by Grissom

A brief explanation:

- In the **core,** you will mainly find individual work, which does not require collaboration, but there can of course be contact with colleagues.

---

[13] https://regarding365.com/where-work-gets-done-8d1d653ef48d

- The **second ring** is mainly for teamwork, where coordination and collaboration in a team, (project) group or department are central.
- The **third ring** is for organisation-wide information, communication, and social interaction.
- Finally, **the outer ring** is where you communicate and collaborate outside the organisation.

Our main criticism of Grissom's overview is that it is all about Microsoft 365. As if there are no other applications at all outside of Microsoft's tools in which communication and collaboration take place. That is of course not true. But we do see this as a good approach to plot all your relevant applications in your organisation, including those of the Microsoft 365 line, in order to provide clarity for management (decision makers) and employees.

Dimension: frequency of use

We derive the second dimension of digital work and collaboration in a digital workplace from Sam Marshall[14], who indicates that employees always have one or more systems open, but that these can be quite different systems, depending on the function they have. In addition, there are systems that employees use regularly and other systems that they only use very occasionally.

---

[14] https://www.clearbox.co.uk/the-myth-of-the-digital-workplace-hub

9 Box Matrix

Combining the two dimensions — type of work and frequency of use — creates a matrix with nine cells, the 9 Box Matrix:

- Horizontally the **dimension type of work:** individual work, in a group or as part of the total organisation.
- Vertically the **dimension frequency of use**: always open, regular use, or incidental use.

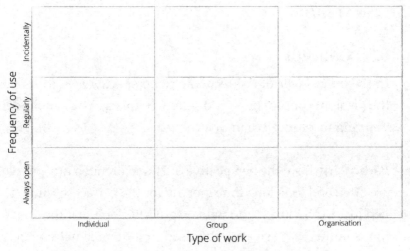

Figure 15: 9 Box Matrix for the digital workplace

The 9 Box Matrix in Figure 15 is intended to plot tasks of different (groups of) employees and the systems they use for these tasks. The matrix can thus provide insight into various cases, for example:

- Which employee groups (persona) (can) perform which tasks with the help of which systems.
- How much overlap and difference there is between the use by diverse groups and which systems are therefore more crucial in an organisation than others.
- What overlap there is between systems and what choices/bottlenecks this causes for employees.

Later in this chapter we will show a concrete application of the 9 Box Matrix.

6.3 Concept

In the outer layer of the technology perspective, we focus on the (design) concept of your digital workplace. You can model your digital workplace in diverse ways.

Particularly from the perspective of IT and architecture, people are often and for a long time looking for the perfect solution. IT vendors in all kinds of domains regularly claim that they have that solution, but we are convinced that there is not one best solution for all organisations. It is precisely when technology comes into focus that the complexity of the whole becomes clear, simply because it is about more than 'just' a system. Hopefully, we will help you on your way with a number of concepts.

6.3.1 Concept 1: landscape

Every organisation now has what you might call the landscape concept: a palette of standalone tools, applications, information sources and channels. So, you already have a digital workplace, as we indicated in the first paragraph of this chapter.

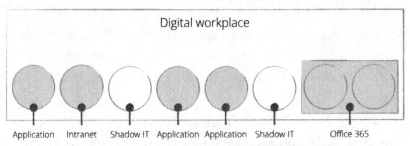

Figure 16: Schematic representation of the digital workplace according to the landscape concept

A digital workplace based on this concept has the important advantage that you can easily and quickly replace applications over time as better alternatives become available on the market. This benefits the sustainability of the concept in the longer term.

The disadvantage of this concept is that there is no main entrance and that employees sometimes do not know (any longer) where they can find which information or perform which action. As a result, people may avoid the 'official' tools and start using their own solutions (shadow IT), which causes the landscape to become more diffuse.

Speaking of shadow IT, a fun fact: As far back as 2015, CIOs said that a third to half of all IT systems in their organisations were made up of shadow IT. Nearly two-thirds of organisations also support those shadow systems in one way or another.

6.3.2 Concept 2: universal

This concept consists of one overarching environment in which you can find news, book holidays, reserve a meeting room, order a new telephone, and consult customer information. The universal concept also solves the issue of that one main entrance. People often think and talk about so-called 'portals' as universal solutions for intranet and the digital workplace.

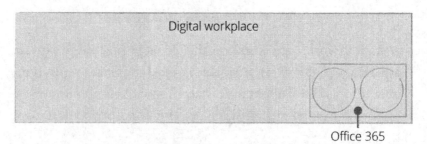

Figure 17: Schematic representation of the digital workplace
according to the universal concept

Although organisations seemed to strive for this (especially in the past) — and Microsoft also seems to want to move to this (again) with Office 365 and MS Teams in particular — such a universal environment does not exist at all. This is a utopia. For both the short term (a lot of design, customisation and therefore not quickly available) and the long term (inflexible, difficult to manage, expensive) such a universal digital workplace is also unworkable.

6.3.3   Concept 3: hybrid

In our experience, many organisations therefore opt for a hybrid solution: a combination of a central (sometimes traditional, more often social) intranet or a portal with a series of applications that were already there anyway. This solution provides the main entrance that is relevant to many employees, without closing side and back doors (to other applications). After all:

- A sales representative will still work directly in the CRM system with customer data.
- A nurse still primarily uses the electronic patient record system.
- And a teacher or student, for example, often works with educational applications such as Canvas.

In addition, according to this concept, a digital workplace with such a central intranet can, on the one hand, accommodate important content and (rich) collaboration. On the other hand, it can integrate commonly used functions of critical but outdated legacy applications by serving as a friendly front end for those applications. Such a central intranet can therefore be more than 'just' a portal.

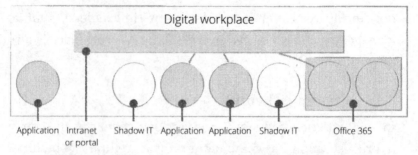

*Figure 18: Schematic representation of the digital workplace
according to the hybrid concept*

The hybrid concept:

- Makes it possible to unlock content and functionality of outdated systems (if only partially) on mobile devices.
- Is flexible in design, which makes it easy to gradually replace outdated systems with newer, better applications, without having to completely change the whole environment.
- Does justice to the broad digital employee experience. After all, there will always be more than one application in the digital workplace, and employee journeys often affect more than one system.
- Gives space to shadow IT and thus allows good shadow solutions to be embraced and supported over time.

In short: if your organisation now has a landscape (and you have one) then a hybrid solution is the only logical next step.

In other words, a workable solution for the digital workplace, and especially for DEX, can really only be a hybrid solution.

6.4   Microsoft 365 in your digital workplace

Almost all organisations we work for already use (part of) Microsoft 365 or have plans to use it. Because of the rapid and widespread emergence, additionally powered by the introduction of MS Teams, we therefore pay some attention to it in this chapter.

Microsoft 365 is not one solution, but rather a line of services — including the well-known Microsoft Office products — that Microsoft brought (and sells!) together under one name. The line consists of dozens of individual, different applications, and services. The line is still growing, applications and services change quite often, some expire, others are being replaced by another product. Some 365 products are quite intuitive and easy to use, but for others the learning curve is very high. This affects usage and adoption of Microsoft 365 in many organisations.

We experience that employees have just gotten used to a certain tool for a specific task and suddenly the tool looks different again and they have lost their information and their buttons. If that happens once, it is not a big deal, but if it happens all the time, people get tired of it.

In addition, we also see the overlap between various applications and services, which makes it sometimes difficult to determine which tool is best to use for what, when and with whom. Moreover, there is sometimes good integration between applications in the line, but sometimes not at all, so that you as an organisation also have to make clear choices yourself what to use in which situation.

Get a grip on Microsoft 365
To find your way around Microsoft 365, various experts offer tools and models to get a grip on the total line of services. We name three:

1. One of the best-known tools is *Matt Wade's The Periodic Table of Microsoft 365*. We think it is a nice overview, but it still has a very high degree of 'here's everything'.
2. Earlier in this chapter we introduced the overview of Brad Grissom 'Where work gets done'. So, it was originally only made for the Microsoft 365 suite, but we have shown that you can give it a broader interpretation.
3. James Robertson has developed a clear management model for Microsoft 365 based on speed versus complexity[15]. This model can help you decide between different strategies for different services in de 365 line.

---

[15] https://www.Steptwo.com.au/papers/management-model-office-365/

6.5 Microsoft 365 ≠ digital workplace

Microsoft 365 can likely never facilitate all processes of your organisation. Think of your CRM, HR, or financial systems. And that makes Microsoft 365 'just' part of a broader digital workplace. We tried to make this clear earlier in the following picture:

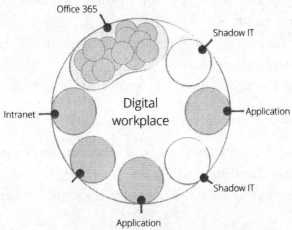

Figure 19: Schematic representation of the positioning of Microsoft 365 in the digital workplace

6.6 What about intranet?

Then there is the old, familiar intranet. That was never the entire digital workplace and never will be. But if an intranet can never be the digital workplace, what is the place of intranet in the whole? That depends on the purposes of your digital workplace, the(design) concept you choose and, for example, what role Microsoft 365 plays. With those things in mind, your intranet can serve as:

- Main entrance to (the rest of) the digital workplace.
- Organisation-wide search and find (including central navigation).
- The central place for (top-down) news and corporate communication.
- Repository for more general information and reference (content management).
- Hub for tasks, features, and notifications from other applications.

If we go one step further, we can of course use the 9 Box Matrix, which we introduced earlier in this chapter, as a guide to determine the role of your intranet in the digital workplace.

What type of work takes place in which box of this matrix? Which applications are appropriate for this? And what place does the intranet occupy? We highlight a few:

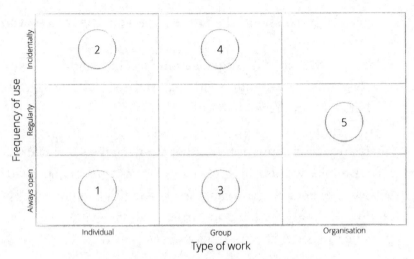

Figure 20: 9 Box Matrix with some examples

1. In the **box solo–always open** a lot of daily work takes place. The question is whether the intranet plays a role here. Maybe when it comes to finding people — one of the important intranet-related tasks in most organisations.

2. In the **box solo–occasionally,** you can think of infrequent tasks and activities. If we think of the intranet, the search could play a role here. But this concerns a broader search than 'just' in the intranet alone, namely searching and finding in multiple systems (enterprise search).

3. The **box group–always open** contains collaboration systems. Think of Teams or Slack, but of course also chat and group functionality on (social) intranets.

4. In the **box group–occasionally** there may be an option to order products via intranet: flower for a colleague's birthday, or printed matter, like a brochure. But it could

also be professional literature that you can access via intranet.

5. The boxes in the **organisation** section could contain corporate news, both incidental and regular, as well as initiatives in the field of *working out loud.*

There are various options for further applying the 9 Box Matrix. For example, we use it to plot specific tasks and associated systems per persona. You can also expand this even further by adding smiling, frowning and frustrated smileys to map the persona's experience with tasks and systems[16].

---

[16] We got this last idea from Marie-Louise Kramer Valsted during the IntraTeam Event 2021 Vol. 3.

"I'm trying to free your mind, Neo.
But I can only show you the door.
You're the one who has to walk through it".
— Morpheus (The Matrix)

7 The autonomy of remote working

By April 2020, about half of the world's population was under some form of lockdown, with more than 3.9 billion people in more than ninety countries or territories having been asked or ordered to stay at home by their governments[17].

The shutdown of workplaces as a measure to control the spread of the COVID-19 virus triggered a mass shift to working from home. When employees were sent home from their offices, many businesses rushed to adopt technology solutions to enable their teams to work remotely. The differences between organisations and the facilities offered were large. In addition, the widespread closure of schools, forced many parents to combine remote working with childcare and home schooling. This took a great toll on people.

In the first period of the pandemic, many people still thought that everyone would soon go back to the office, but the reality turned out to be more unruly. Governments called repeatedly for people to continue working from home as much as possible to minimise travel and contact.

---

[17] https://www.euronews.com/2020/04/02/coronavirus-in-europe-spain-s-death-toll-hits-10-000-after-record-950-new-deaths-in-24-hou

Meanwhile, a dichotomy arose. Between people who wanted to get back to the office as soon as possible and others who thrived at home. In the first group, for that matter, home education of (young) children probably also played a part, because that naturally has a massive impact. The question is how you as an organisation can respond to developments as effectively as possible.

We believe that working and communicating remotely offers new opportunities. We do not intend to convince everyone that this is the way, but we do want to make you think about things that seem obvious, but may not be. What suits your organisation and especially diverse groups of employees in your organisation?

7.1 The DEX of remote working

Remote working offers organisations new, additional possibilities to tailor work and communication more closely to the unique needs of individual employees. Precisely by looking at this from the (digital) employee experience, opportunities arise to personalise work: from one size fits all to custom fit.

What motivates people to do their job (well)?
In his book *Drive* (2009), Daniel Pink describes three elements, based on the Self-determination theory, that (intrinsically) motivate us as people in our work and that can lead to professional success and personal satisfaction:

- **Autonomy:** the desire to be self-directed, to control your own life and work.
- **Mastery**: the desire to get better and better at something that matters to you.
- **Purpose**: the desire to do something that has meaning, and is part of something larger than yourself.

The three elements are almost inextricably linked. According to Pink: """Autonomous people who strive for mastery perform at an exceedingly high level. But those who do so in the service of a higher purpose can achieve even more". Pink does indicate that the elements mainly apply to non-routine tasks, for which you need creativity and problem-solving skills, for example. Routine tasks are more likely to rely on external motivators, such as money.

7.2 Personalisation of work

Back to remote working, where there is a direct relationship with the autonomy of the employee. Autonomy gives people control over:

- their **task**: what they do
- their **time**: when they do the task
- their **team**: with whom they do the task
- and their **technique/approach**: how they do the task

We previously mentioned this as the opportunity to personalise your work. Personalisation concerns, on the one hand, the possibility to use your own devices and software to work within the office environment. On the other hand, personalisation is also increasingly the possibility to work remotely at a desired location, and for example also at a desired time.

Bricks and mortar not needed for autonomy
Matt Mullenweg, founder of Automattic (best known for developing WordPress), describes five levels of distributed work[18]. Mullenweg prefers the term 'distributed' to 'remote', because the latter implies that there is still a central workplace. Automattic employs nearly 2,000 employees, spread all over the world, without a joint office.

Daniel Pink's work has inspired Mullenweg in the development of Automattic. According to Mullenweg, mastery and purpose are also well expressed in 'physical' companies, but when it comes to autonomy, even the best-in-office company can never perform better than a distributed company. He illustrates this as follows:

"Now imagine an environment where you can choose and control every one of those to your liking — maybe it's a room in your house, a converted garage, a shared studio, or really anything, the important thing is you're able to shape the environment fit your personal preferences, not the lowest

---

[18] https://ma.tt/2020/04/five-levels-of-autonomy

common denominator of everyone an employer has decided to squish together for 8 hours a day."

The description is somewhat exaggerated, but Mullenweg is right when he says that many (basic) elements in the office environment are beyond our control. Think of the temperature, specific scents, type of desk, if you have window view, available food, and so on. These elements can all influence the extent to which you give and receive (creative) energy.

7.3   Five levels of autonomy

Mullenweg's *Distributed Work's Five Levels of Autonomy* model actually consists of six levels. But the first level is level 0, on which you can only perform a task if you are physically present on site. Think of the work of firefighters, bricklayers, nurses, and production workers on the assembly line.

Incidentally, digital communication and collaboration can also be relevant for these target groups. Moreover, we expect that, based on the various technological innovations, major developments will take place for these groups in the coming years. As we also described in the perspective of the physical environment in Chapter 4.

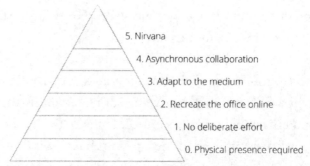

Figure 21: Distributed Work's Five Levels of Autonomy by Mullenweg

7.3.1 Level 1: No deliberate effort

At the first level, the organisation has not made any deliberate efforts to make things remotely friendly. Employees (mostly only knowledge workers) can do some work from home or another location for a day or two if it is really necessary. For this they might have a smartphone with access to their e-mail and calendar. Most things must wait until employees get back to the office. "Work happens on company equipment, in company space, on company time", according to Mullenweg.

This makes remote working a rather weak alternative to working in the office. Some organisations were at this level before the COVID-19 outbreak and were therefore not really prepared for what was to come.

7.3.2 Level 2: Recreate the office online

Employees have access to videoconferencing tools like Zoom and Microsoft Teams at this level. But the "old" way of working – for example working between 9 and 5 — is preserved rather than redesigning the work to take advantage of digital innovations.

This also perpetuates and sometimes even reinforces all bad office habits online. Think of ten-person video calls where two people are enough, more than sixty interruptions a day — now via Slack or Yammer, for example — checking and answering email multiple times a day, and the continuous hyper-responsiveness expected from employees.

All activities are still synchronous (at the same time), no real-time meetings have been cancelled and there is a lot of management anxiety around (lack of) productivity. Many organisations are currently still at this level.

7.3.3   Level 3: Adapt to the medium

At level 3, organisations start to adapt to and benefit from the new possibilities of remote or distributed work. Think of shared documents (such as a Google documents) that are visible to everyone and are updated in real time during a discussion. This immediately creates a shared understanding of what has been discussed and decided and there is no need to make a report afterwards, which also needs to be checked.

With this, more robust, asynchronous processes begin to replace meetings. Effective written communication becomes critical as organisations embrace remote working. In addition, there is a preference for more asynchronous communication (in

Chapter 9 we go into this in more detail). At this level, organisations also start to invest in better equipment for their employees, such as noise cancelling headphones.

Finally, the organisation (if there is no pandemic), organises a few meetings per year where employees can meet in person in a relaxed atmosphere. The office becomes more like a clubhouse for connecting and interacting with your colleagues.

7.3.4   Level 4: Embrace asynchronous collaboration

I read it or respond to it when it suits me: this is the nature of asynchronous communication and collaboration that characterises fourth-level organisations. Most activities do not require an immediate response at all, even if you want to collaborate effectively. A one-way email or instant message may be enough, and the recipient will reply when it is most suitable. If something is urgent, you can pick up the phone.

Asynchronous communication gives employees more time to think, create and get into a flow state that makes them more productive. At the same time, it provides the opportunity for various kinds of people to take (perhaps slower, but more deliberate) decisions. It allows anyone — not just the most extroverted — to join the conversation and decide on important topics.

In addition, asynchronous communication offers flexibility to night owls to start their working day later, as long as there is a reasonable overlap with the working time of early birds. When you collaborate asynchronously, you show that you respect other people's time and focus.

Organisations that have truly made asynchronous communication and collaboration the standard way of working have gone beyond the industrial revolution. They no longer combine presence with productivity. Because of this they also have the advantage of being able to make use of the global talent pool, "the 99% of the world's population and intelligence that does not live near one of your legacy physical office location".

In addition, organisations can be truly inclusive, because standards are much more objective and give people the opportunity to do their work in their own way. According to Mullenweg his company Automattic is at this level.

7.3.5   Level 5: 'Nirvana'

Level 5 is the ideal image, which according to Mullenweg cannot be fully realised, but is always good to aim for. At this level, the distributed organisation performs better than any 'traditional' organisation could ever do. As an employee you can be effortlessly effective. Everything, both the culture of the organisation, as well as the physical and technological environment, supports you in every way. It is when all employees have enough time for well-being and mental health, try to be their best selves, as creative as possible and get the best out of their careers and just have fun!

7.4   Getting started with (even) more autonomy

The autonomy pyramid indicates what the growth opportunities are when it comes to remote, distributed working. It was fairly easy for Mullenweg, because he could build Automattic from scratch according to his own preferences: completely remote and distributed from the start. He was also able to recruit and hire only people that also wanted to work this way.

Nevertheless, we think that the model can also inspire existing organisations to really start working differently, give employees more autonomy and thus contribute to a better digital employee experience in the broadest sense.

As indicated, organisations start to really benefit from distributed working from level 3 onwards. However, various organisations are still at level 2. Because working from home is definitely here to stay, it can be interesting and valuable for organisations and employees to move from level 2 (Recreate the office online) to level 3 (Adapt to the medium). At the same time also looking further ahead at the principles and possibilities of level 4 (Embrace asynchronous collaboration).

There is a direct connection between more flexibility in working conditions and employee satisfaction and happiness. This immediately provides benefits for employees, but also for the organisation. By giving employees more autonomy, you create a more pleasant work environment. This helps to reduce stress and staff turnover.

7.5   Working remote or hybrid

As we described in chapter 4, we see some differences between the Dutch and international situation. In 2020, several international companies already announced that they would permanently switch to remote working.

Although many Dutch people expect to work from home more often, for most the office seems to remain the home base for the time being. Organisations in the Netherlands are now focusing on hybrid work, combining work from home with working on location, in alignment with the wishes of many employees.

This new situation will certainly require a lot of extra brainwork, because it is more complex than Automattic's starting position. We think the past period has been 'easy' compared to what will come next. During the pandemic everybody has worked more or less under the same conditions, for example with equal access to information. One of the hardest things in hybrid work will be to keep this equality between remote and in-office workers.

8 Culture of digital work and collaboration

For years, we have been reading and hearing success stories from people, teams, and organisations that work and collaborate digitally using various digital tools. But we hear and read just as many stories about failed initiatives, sometimes with the same tools.

In chapter 7 we introduced Mullenweg's autonomy pyramid. This model shows that the more you work distributed and remotely as an organisation, the more autonomy you give your employees. But how do you actually do that, successfully work, and collaborate, in a remote or even distributed way?

8.1 More than working from home

How we work from home during COVID-19 is not necessarily the same as effective digital work and collaboration, although this is often suggested. Digital work and collaboration appear to be a lot of video conferencing at this moment. We simply replace the formal and informal conversations that we normally have at the same place and time, face-to-face, with digital variants. Of course, we do not have the conversations in the same place, but we often have them at the same time: the well-known meeting culture between 9 and 5, unfortunately now also online. You just no longer have to look for an empty meeting place, because there is plenty of room...

8.2 Work independently of time and place

Not only is there a difference between working from home and working digitally. There is also difference between place-independent work — many people have been doing this from home since spring 2020 — and time-independent work. This is still rare. In other words, we do work in various places, but still mainly at the same time, or synchronously.

Synchronous collaboration means that people connect and work together at the same time. They talk using a video call in Zoom, collaborate simultaneously in an online document in Google Drive or hold a joint brainstorm session with (digital) sticky notes in Mural. A chat conversation in, for example, Microsoft Teams is also a form of synchronous collaboration, when people have the expectation that a response will be (very) quickly.

Asynchronous collaboration means that you do not expect an immediate response (or even no response at all). For example, when you share what you did that day in an intranet message, and a colleague who works on other days reads that message and therefore responds later. Or if you send a large document using WeTransfer to a number of external collaboration partners.

You can also use some of the tools we mentioned in synchronous collaboration for asynchronous collaboration. For example, a chat conversation can extend over several days or sometimes you respond the same day. You can also work on documents asynchronously with colleagues. Finally, asynchronous online brainstorming can be especially useful if you want input from many people, not all of whom are available at the same time.

8.3   Working asynchronously in your organisation?

Even after COVID-19, work will increasingly in various places and no longer exclusively at offices in city centres. As a result, people spend less time together, which can also lead to an increase in meeting culture. Video conferencing has replaced those meetings.

However, asynchronous communication and collaboration are more practical in many cases. People can decide for themselves at what moment they take in certain information, when they respond and when they make their contribution This will also improve their contribution, as it is less ad hoc and under less time pressure. They also have more time for focused work, which can lead to increased productivity.

Of course, there must also be room for synchronous meetings, but this can be done less often and at the same time more efficiently or more pleasantly (depending on the goal). Such meetings require good preparation. The advantage of asynchronous communication and collaboration is that more is immediately recorded, in systems, in any way. This ensures that more input, context, and background information is available, so that you can go directly in-depth during a (limited number of) meetings and have more impact together.

Working asynchronously also offers other advantages. For example, think of more flexibility and a better work-life balance.

Primary school best practise

We have seen for ourselves that the combination of synchronous and asynchronous can really work in practice. In this case, a best practise from 2020 at a primary school where the teacher posted the day schedule for the whole week online on a 'Padlet' (a kind of digital bulletin board).

In addition to assignments for spelling, arithmetic, history, and coding, the padlet also includes links to specific tutorials on YouTube and downloadable assignments in Word. The children could easily upload their assignments to the padlet themselves and received feedback from the teacher. And especially likes from the other children. Separate padlets were made for projects, for example about World War II, and

---

the children were also given the task of making their own project padlet.

Finally, the padlet contained links to some scheduled (mandatory and non-mandatory) meetings in Microsoft Teams. These meetings were used for making agreements as well as for instruction. They were also used for fun things like digital Easter egg hunts and dancing together to the latest hits.

By being online together in this way at planned, synchronous moments and alternating this with asynchronous assignments, the teacher could keep a close eye on whether all children were still on schedule. The children also had contact with each other and at the same time they could work on assignments at their own pace every week. This best practices can be translated in many ways to the work and (digital) workplace of adults.

Clear agreements required
As we described earlier, working asynchronously requires that you make clear agreements with each other. This approach requires a great deal of independence and discipline from employees in exchange for the freedom to determine where, when, and how you work.

GitLab, the world's largest all-remote organisation with more than 1,300 employees in more than sixty-five countries, has made asynchronous working the standard, as stated in their 'Remote Manifesto'. Seven of the nine principles of this manifesto are relevant for digital work and collaboration:

- Flexible working hours (over set working hours).
- Writing down and recording knowledge (over verbal explanations).
- Written processes (over on-the-job training).
- Public sharing of information (over need-to-know access).
- Opening documents for editing by anyone (over top-down control of documents).
- Asynchronous communication (over synchronous communication).
- Formal communication channels (over informal communication channels).

Do you want to know more about working remotely by default? Then we strongly recommend that you read the information that GitLab publishes and get inspired.[19]

8.4   More than working with digital tools

Digital work and collaboration are different from doing your work using digital tools. Jan van Ginkel also stated this in a weblog on iBestuur in April 2020:[20] "Yes, we are certainly

[19] https://about.gitlab.com/company/culture/all-remote/guide
[20] https://ibestuur.nl/weblog/verwekt-in-april

quickly becoming more skilled with digital tools and the roll-out of new digital tools at government and at local authorities this can now be done in a week instead of through a year-long implementation plan — all fantastic of course — but that has little to do with digital transformation. What we now only see is that the work is being organised more digitally. But it is still the existing work, the existing services, the existing logic".

To be successful in digital work and collaboration, we need to design new ways of working. These new ways of working are about letting go of existing practices, processes and resources and asking yourself what the purpose of your work is. Once that is clear, you might be able to accomplish that goal of your work in a different, better way, using other digital tools.

8.5 Why does it sometimes work and sometimes not?

We return to the question we already asked in the introduction to this chapter: why do some organisations succeed in digital work and collaboration and others fail, while using the same tools?

All this has to do with the communication and collaboration style in your organisation and the idea behind the use of certain digital tools. To clarify this, we use Cameron & Quinn's Competing Values Framework, a well-known model for categorising organisational cultures. The model is derived from empirical research into which factors make organisations effective. [21]

Cameron & Quinn distinguish two (value) dimensions for categorising organisational culture:

Figure 22: Competing Values Framework by Cameron & Quinn

- **Stability versus flexibility**: some organisations strive for stability and internal control of processes by describing, measuring, monitoring, and continuously improving processes. At the same time, other organisations want to

---

[21]

https://en.wikipedia.org/wiki/Organizational_culture#Kim_Cameron_and_Robert_Quinn

be flexible to be able to respond as quickly as possible to opportunities that arise. This also has an impact on the way organisations deal with information, communication and collaboration and what kind of digital systems they use. re these systems primarily focused on stability and control, or do they offer flexibility and opportunities to share information and knowledge?

- **Internal versus external orientation**: organisations have a predominant internal or external focus. Organisations with an internal orientation focus on integration, collaboration, and unity. While organisations with an external orientation focus on differentiation, competition, and rivalry. This also has consequences for digital work and collaboration. Do methods, procedures and systems have to match the existing situation in the organisation? Or does the organisation mainly focus on new opportunities and opportunities?

Together, the dimensions form four quadrants, each with its own set of indicators for organisational effectiveness:

Hierarchy

The hierarchy culture is characterised by a highly formalised and structured work environment in which everything is in control. Procedures determine what people do and everything revolves around formal agreements and standards to keep the organisation stable and sustainable. Success is defined in terms of reliable delivery, smooth planning, and low costs. The first described organisations, from the 1950s, contain characteristics of this culture.

Market

From the late 1960s, when organisations faced new challenges in the competitive environment, the market-oriented culture became popular. This is a very results-oriented work environment, in which competition — also internally between teams and departments — are central. For the long term, the focus is on achieving measurable goals and objectives. Success is defined in terms of market share and market penetration.

Clan

In the late 1970s and early 1980s, a new culture type was discovered by studying Japanese companies. The clan culture in these organisations focused on common values and goals and the relationships between people (both employees and customers). The organisation attaches immense importance to teamwork, participation, and consensus. Success is defined in terms of working atmosphere and caring for people.

Adhocracy

The adhocracy culture emerged with the transition from the industrial to the information age. Such organisations have a dynamic, entrepreneurial, and creative work environment, which reacts strongly to changes in the environment that are characteristic of the twenty-first century. Employees step up and dare to take risks. The glue that holds the organisation together is a sense of commitment to experimentation and innovation. Success means delivering unique and original products and thus leading the way.

Based on the descriptions of the quadrants, a number of names of companies and organisations probably come to mind. At the same time, (especially larger) organisations can have characteristics from different quadrants, depending on, for example, the department or field in which you work. But Cameron and Quinn indicate that effective organisations almost always have a dominant culture.

With the *Organisational Culture Assessment Instrument (OCAI)*[22] you can gain more insight into the current and desired organisational culture of your own organisation. Please note, diagnosis should be a joint activity of key figures from different organisational levels and preferably also the environment. Moreover, the process is just as important as the result. Discussing current and desired values can be a cultural intervention in itself.

8.6 (Digital) collaboration and culture

If you look at the different quadrants, you probably already see that some digital tools fit more naturally with certain culture types and organisational characteristics. Tools and

---

[22] https://www.ocai-online.com/

functionalities that stimulate connection between people, such as enterprise social networks (with features like posting, following, and liking messages) and profiles and groups on your (social) intranet fit well with a family culture. While in such a culture, sharing and searching documents through a comprehensive document management system with version control is likely to encounter great resistance.

This contrasts with the hierarchy culture, in which this fits extremely well and effectively contributes to more stability and control. In turn, it is necessary for organisations with an innovative, adhocracy culture to quickly test new ideas in the market on social media or even to develop them jointly in co-creation with customers and partners, for example with visual brainstorming and collaboration tools. But organisations with a market-oriented culture are all about maintaining a strong competitive position with the help of a CRM system, in which employees actively keep track of customer information. Sharing creative ideas quickly is just not done.

These examples make it clear why you cannot just deploy a digital collaboration tool in another organisation with the same success. The more the concept and operation of the tool are in line with your organisational culture, the easier, more pleasant, and productive employees will use it in their daily work.

8.7   Tools do not change culture

We often hear that new collaboration tools are seen as a means to change the culture in an organisation, because 'people have no choice but to change with the tools'. In our experience, it is extremely difficult to change people's behaviour in this way. If cultural change is desired, collaboration tools can support the necessary movement, but only if they are combined with a clear vision and goals, change of leadership style, recognition and appreciation of employees and an appropriate training policy. Matters that we have already described in chapter 4 as an important part of the DEX Model.

9 Opportunities for personalised communication

Appreciation for internal communication has increased in 2020 under the influence of COVID-19. More leaders see the value in internal communication and how it helps companies navigate change, according to Forbes[23]. We believe this offers opportunities to take the next steps.

Communication plays a significant role in all levels of the autonomy pyramid from Chapter 7, but especially in the transition from level 2 (Recreate the office online) to 3 (Adapt to the medium) and from level 3 to 4 (Embrace asynchronous collaboration). Communication can be both the connecting factor — after all, the Latin word *communicare* means 'to share, or to make common' — and it can contribute to more personalisation options and therefore also autonomy for individual employees.

We see a more extensive role for (internal) communication professionals, as Logeion (Dutch Association for Communication) also announced at the end of 2020. [24] "More than ever, internal communication is important to keep the

---

[23] https://www.forbes.com/sites/forbesagencycouncil/2020/07/16/the-moment-of-truth-for-internal-communications/?sh=31d8c1854462
[24] https://www.logeion.nl/trends-2020-2021

company together. And to keep employees going. Involving employees in realising the ambitions of your organisation is normally already difficult. But it is even more complicated when you work remote. It requires insight into the wishes of managers and employees, it requires finding the right balance in communication and it also requires personal communication. "

Now that so many things are changing, it is important to think about various aspects of internal communication and to make clear agreements. Then everyone knows what the options are and what to expect. We get a lot of inspiration from 'The Basecamp Guide to Internal Communication', that provides an extensive view on 'the how, where, why and when we communicate' for people that work at Basecamp. In our opinion topics you should at least think about are:

- Physical and digital communication.
- Formal and informal communication.
- Synchronous and asynchronous communication.
- Fast and slow communication.

9.1 Physical and digital communication

When you compare physical and digital communication, personal preferences immediately arise. It is not obvious which colleagues find more pleasant. Many people long to meet and talk to colleagues in person (again). We hear from more introverted people that they really enjoy the lack of physical meetings, and value digital communication, especially via text, over video calling. They thrive on working and communicating digitally. Employees should have more opportunities to make an individual choice in this regard, within the agreed organisational and communication policy.

9.2 Formal and informal communication

In the transition from the office to working from home, we initially saw a lot of attention for formal communication and consultation. Regarding formal communication, a golden tip: never, ever use a meeting to simply pass on information. That is what email or chat is for. (All those "important" meetings are indeed reduced to emails.)

In addition to formal communication, attention has gradually been paid to more informal communication. In May 2020, in a broadcast by the Utrecht Communication Circle (UCK) [25], it was also concluded that more (formal) internal communication is not the solution to overcome social cohesion in distributed forms of working. On the contrary, it is important to organise more explicitly the informal contact that arises more or less by chance in a workplace, school, or office environment.

---

[25]https://www.communicatiekring.nl/k/n107/news/view/5621/2072/ wegvallen-sociale-cohesie-los-je-niet-op-met-meer-interne- communicatie.html l

The proverbial coffee machine — and sometimes it is not a coffee machine at all, but a water cooler, a kitchenette or something completely different — must have a digital version. The advantages of a 'digital coffee machine' include:

- Colleagues can bond with each other.
- Spontaneous interaction can bring new ideas.
- A shared place to meet informally can enhance the sense of belonging.

GitLab, which we mentioned earlier, also published about how they deal with informal communication in their all-remote teams and takes this a few steps further. It is good to think about which options you deliberately facilitate as an organisation that suit your organisational goals and the needs of your employees. Above all, encourage employees to develop initiatives themselves and think also about how to maintain these new practices as an organisation.

In chapter 4 we already mention augmented and virtual reality as technical innovations in the physical domain. Virtual reality can offer all kinds of new possibilities for informal connection between people.

The virtual chat service Mibo shows this clearly. With Mibo you can, for example, have a virtual drink or hang out with your team. The chat service combines video calling with a 3D world, which we know from the game world. Your screen shows in Mibo as the head of a computer character that can walk around on a tropical island for example.

Thanks to positional audio, you only hear the voice of people who are close to you. If a colleague walks up to you, his or her voice starts to sound closer. So, just like at a real drink, you can walk around to talk to different colleagues.

In addition, you can sit together on cushions or chairs, there are caps and hats to make teams, you can play the piano in the saloon and there is even a treasure hidden that you can search for together.

9.3 Synchronous and asynchronous communication

As we saw in the description of level 4 in the autonomy pyramid, asynchronous communication allows you to match the work rhythm of individual employees much better. By default, organisations are more geared towards early birds. With asynchronous communication you also meet night owls. This gives both groups maximum flexibility. It is important that there is sufficient (time) overlap between different groups of employees who need each other. If your organisation works across multiple time zones, you already know this is not easy. Clear (communication) agreements are also necessary for this. To really move forward with asynchronous communication, let us take a look again at Basecamp's internal communication guide, which includes all kinds of principles that make communication explicit, such as:

- If you want an answer, you have to ask a question.
- If your words can be perceived in different ways, they'll be understood in the way which does the most harm.
- If you have to repeat yourself, you were not clear enough the first time. However, if you are talking about something brand new, you may have to repeat yourself for years before you are heard. Pick your repeats wisely.

Basecamp (of course) uses its own system for automated asynchronous communication support. This also provides inspiration. Think, for example, of the 'automatic daily': every employee gets the question 'What did you work on today?' Everything people write up is shared with the rest of the organisation. This is to support 'loose accountability and strong reflection'. Some employees just write down a few bullet points. Others write more in diary style. There are no requirements, everyone writes according to their own needs.

9.4 Fast and slow communication

A large part of the principles from the Basecamp guide is about paying sufficient attention to communication and calmness in communication. This fits well with Simon Terry's push and pull communication framework[26]. Terry argues that we place too much value on fast communication and one hundred percent reach and adoption (push). While it is far more productive to let employees retrieve the information when and where they need (pull). For example, with an internal social network.

Terry also refers to Daniel Kahneman, author of *Thinking Fast and Slow*. Kahneman won a Nobel Prize in Economics for his Prospect Theory, which states that we give (potential) loss much more weight than (potential) gain. Terry links this to push communication, which we know is often ineffective, but which we continue to use, because we are concerned about the disaster that will befall us if not everyone has received the relevant information.

But Kahneman's theory also shows that communication and collaboration within a network can yield exponential returns: a small, well-connected group of individuals can achieve enormous performance improvements.

---

[26] https://simonterry.com/2020/04/15/pull-push-fast-and-slow-part-i

10 *The Matrix*: The End of Digital Illusions?

At the end of this book, we have a choice. The choice between a red and a blue pill. Just like Neo, the main character in the 1999 film *The Matrix*. Rebel leader Morpheus gives him the choice to take the blue pill and return to a physically comatose existence in a liquid-filled pod and to live in a pleasant shared simulated reality, the Matrix. Or to take the red pill and wake up from this digital nightmare and defeat the machines that keep the Matrix alive.

We can also continue to marvel at all the digital vistas. A bit like in chapter 2 where we looked ahead from 2010 to a working day in 2020 with all the digital conveniences that entail: say the blue pill. Or we opt for the red pill and take the basics of Josh Bersin's work as a starting point: being able to express and share your talents, receive fair treatment, have the opportunity to learn and grow, get recognition for what you do and feel safe in your work environment.

That will certainly not be easy, but it sounds like it is worth it. We hope this book on digital employee experience and our DEX model will contribute to that.

10.1 DEX Reloaded

In the introduction of this book, we already mentioned Robertson's definitions of digital employee experience and a (great) digital workplace. In this concluding chapter, with the basics of Bersin in mind, we add the following and further reload DEX:

- A **great digital employee experience** is the sum of all digital interactions in a work environment, **where the needs and expectations of employees come first**.
- Subsequently, a **human digital workplace** offers employees (a coherent set of) tools that contribute to a sense of safety, productivity, and connectedness, offer space for relaxation, and provide the opportunity to optimally collaborate with others and to grow as an employee.

According to Bersin, if you want to make work a better place "you just have to remember the basics". He makes several suggestions on how to do that, which can also be the starting point for a great digital employee experience. And also, more, and better digital work and collaboration, as we have described in various chapters in this book. We will briefly go over them in the following paragraphs.

10.1.1 Freedom to do wonderful things

People work to be able to express their talents and share them with others. They want to do work that they enjoy, that is useful and that they can be proud of. Bersin says: "Give them the opportunity and freedom to do this and they'll do amazing things. "

In chapter 7, we have shown how remote working can offer organisations new, additional opportunities to tailor work and communication more closely to the unique needs of individual employees. We described the five levels of autonomy, which give people more control over their task (what they do), their time (when they do the work), their team (with whom they do the work) and their technique (how they do the work). This can offer employees more opportunities and more freedom to express their talents and share them with others.

10.1.2 Growth and (digital) culture go hand in hand

Bersin indicates that people want to grow in their work. "Give them opportunities to learn, try new things and experiment with their careers, and they'll surprise you with their adaptability. "

From the digital employee experience perspective, we see a strong relationship with the culture in an organisation, which we described in chapter 8. Using the Model of Competing Values, we discussed the influence of organisational culture on the degree of digital work and collaboration and partly vice versa. The Clan culture and Adhocracy culture contain characteristics of learning and experimentation. We believe that in organisations with such cultures, digital work and collaboration will offer opportunities for employees to grow, and to flexibly move along with the wind of change.

10.1.3 Recognition through personalised communication

In chapter 9 we explained various aspects of personal communication. We summarise Bersin's three other basic principles in this paragraph, as we see opportunities here to support his advice with the various forms of personalised communication.

People want ...

- **to be treated fairly**. "Give them a voice", Bersin says. "Include them in decisions, and share information so they know why decisions are made as they are".
- **to be recognised for the contribution they make**. Thank your employees, is one of Bersin's other advices. ".. recognise what they do and listen to what they say. These things create more energy than any bonus or new pay scheme".
- **to feel safe in their work environment**. People want to work in a friendly environment where there is trust. They want to be able to freely express their opinions and "They want to know people won't talk about them behind their back", Bersin says. "And they want to know that leaders are watching out for them every day".

These three basic principles are intricately linked to the feeling and personal perception of the individual employee. It is mainly about how employees experience the organisation, leadership by managers and collaboration with colleagues. Communication plays a significant role in this. When you attune communication as much as possible to personal preferences (digital or physical, formal, or informal, synchronous, or asynchronous and fast or slow) and also use various means of communication (both informative and interactive), employees are given all kinds of opportunities to take note of it, interact with it and influence it in their own way.

10.2 DEX Revolutions: Back to the future again?

The idea that human beings are more and more merging with technology is no longer limited to science fiction films, like The Matrix Revolutions (the last in the trilogy of The Matrix films).

At the end of this book we return to Christiaan, our own Marty McFly in 2010. Back then, he already wrote about the PDA, the personal digital assistant. That is, of course, today's smartphone, which almost everyone has. The market penetration of smartphones in the Netherlands has grown to 95% in 2021[27]. And for the age groups of 18-24 years and 35-44

---

[27] https://www.consultancy.nl/nieuws/33772/nederland-is-koning-smartphone-samsung-groter-dan-apple

years that is even 98%. For knowledge workers, daily work is now also unimaginable without such a device in your pocket or bag.

At the same time, the Christiaan of 2010 could not have foreseen how far many of us have already merged with our smartphones. As an extension of our hand, with which we control the digital and physical world around us. The smartphone is still outside the body, but in the future, it may be embedded in our body or brain, making people and technology inextricably linked.

Let us see how our Marty McFly looks back on the rest of his expectations 10 years later.

***

SOMEWHERE IN NOVEMBER 2020

For a long time, it seemed almost magical: the year 2020. Five to ten years ago, many strategic plans had this year as a dot on the horizon. Many trend watchers and futurists were looking forward to it. Me too. What would the world look like? How would we live? How would we do our job? Which technology would play a role in this?

One inbox for all information flows
The first of my expectations of 2010 was based on a personal wish: one inbox in which all kinds of messages came together: "e-mail, text

messages, voicemails, messages from different social media, DM's and the *latest news*". There is still no such universal inbox. At least, not one where you receive both e-mail and WhatsApp messages and your social media messages from Facebook, LinkedIn and Twitter, and your daily dose of news.

In that respect, the landscape is further fragmented by new channels such as WhatsApp and (social) platforms such as Instagram, although both are of course owned by Facebook and work is also being done on merging Facebook Messenger and WhatsApp.
To be honest, on second thought, I am not mournful that we never got the universal inbox. After all, there is a time and a place for all information flows, and that does not (always) have to be the same place. As far as I am concerned, I would rather not, because that only leads to even more information overload.

A truly personal device
That personal device is, of course, our ever-present smartphone, which we really cannot live without anymore. What was also correct was the 'projecting' of information from your PDA... er, from your smartphone, onto other screens. I am thinking of my Apple TV, but also of the Google Chromecast, of the screens and dongles from of manufacturers like Barco and of smart screens in conference rooms where you can also display your laptop screen wirelessly without (too many) problems.

The principle of bring your own device (BYOD) has also become much more common in recent years. While that was still quite special in 2010, people nowadays increasingly decide for themselves which types of device they use, whether it is a smartphone, tablet, or laptop. In addition, my impression is also that fewer people have two mobile (smart) phones, one for private and one for business use.

What the smartphone is not, or at least limited, is a 'workstation'. Not that you can't communicate, read, collaborate, and video call with your phone — certainly, you can. By 'workstation' I mean that you connect a monitor, keyboard and mouse to your smartphone and then use that the way many knowledge workers now use their tablet and/or laptop. Samsung does have solutions for this in the market, but I've never seen them in real life.

Time and place independent work

Reading and managing your e-mails at home in the morning — even in bed if necessary — was already possible with the arrival of the first smartphones. Whether that's wise, I'll leave it up to you for now. But as a knowledge worker doing your work at home, in the office, with customers and partners, and on the road was already fairly normal, at that time. Some people had even found a very pleasant balance by, for example, working two days at home and two or three days in the office.

What no one could have foreseen in 2010, or expected by the end of 2019, is that COVID-19 completely turned that cautious balance upside down. Working from home was not only encouraged, but more or less expected of knowledge workers. Travel was and is discouraged, and many offices were even (temporarily) closed. In order to be able to continue the work, most organisations resorted to video calling. With all the associated (also negative) consequences. Although I know time and place independent work can be done in many different ways.

Things like biometric security — logging in with, for example, fingerprint or facial scan — have been possible for several years now. But this mainly concerns personal devices (smartphone, laptop). As far as I know, in the office or other work environments this happens little or not at all. In recent years, we have also collectively started to feel less comfortable with this, so I wonder whether this will really become commonplace in the near future.

Documents and other information carriers

Google Docs was the first widely used application that made it easy to work on the same document at the same time. In the meantime, it is also possible in Microsoft Office 365 in a fairly simple way. So, I was right in that regard.

At the time, I had no idea how the digital world would change when it comes to documents as the primary information carrier. Between 2010 and 2018 I got the impression that digital collaboration would increasingly happen with media other than documents. Think of wikis, chat and (other) text-based collaboration tools. They also fit very well with asynchronous work.

My impression is that the rise of Microsoft 365 has ensured that "the document as primary information carrier" is far from disappearing. After all, one of the pillars of Microsoft 365 is working with *documents: SharePoint is all about documents, in Teams a lot happens around documents, and so on. This maintains working with and thinking in documents, while a document is not always the best information carrier.*

At the same time, technology is not only to blame for the fact that we mainly still work and think in documents. Because in many organisations knowledge work is still done according to processes based on documents and filing cabinets. Only now we no longer create and read the documents on paper, but via screens. And we no longer store them in binders in physical cabinets, but in OneDrive, SharePoint, or another document management system.

One more thing about documents: "On the way I listen to the management summary of the project plan: my PDA connects to the intranet for this, converts the document into speech". Virtual assistants are increasingly doing this very well. Now when I'm on the road, I often have saved articles read by Siri. I do that at one and a half times the speed, so I can absorb information faster. The other way around is also getting better: I dictate a (short) message quite regularly via iMessage, WhatsApp or e-mail, especially when I'm on the road.

Smartphone even more important
Finally, I would like to point out the role of the smartphone in and around the house. Because it may have become even stronger than I could have imagined in 2010. Of course, streaming movies and music from your smartphone to a smart speaker, TV or other device has

become quite normal for many people. Smart home solutions for lighting, heating, opening curtains, etc. are also becoming more common. And the smartphone is the 'hub' where all the settings for the smart home come together.

In 2010, I also had no idea that your smartphone can also replace your house key and open and start your car. That you can pay with it at just about all stores. And that it has become a crucial tool for sports and personal health, especially in combination with a smartwatch. Steve Jobs was really right in that sense when he said: "There's an app for that".

***

A lot was already possible in 2010
Much of what Christiaan envisioned for 2020 at the time was actually already possible in 2010. But even then, we already knew that the limiting factor was not really technology, but rather people.

This has certainly been true in recent years. Digital transformation is not about technology, but much more about digital skills of people, business models, organisational change, culture, *and* focus on the needs of employees. Gradually, more and more attention is being paid to this.

For many organisations, COVID-19 has really accelerated things. For example, the past year has shown that people can handle the responsibility of remote working very well. In general, organisations can rest assured that employees will simply do their job, even if the manager does not monitor them all the time. But the past year has also shown that old ways of working — in the office from meeting to meeting, and now from video conference to video conference — are exhausting. Furthermore, it appears that involvement in the organisation and the perpetuation of the corporate culture can suffer from the physical distance.

We have learned that personal wellbeing, engagement, and culture are even more important than we may have thought. That when employees work independently of place and time, this demands quite different things from organisations and managers than when we used to be in the office between 9 and 5.

In the coming years, we hope and expect that, in addition to growing attention for (even) better digital tools organisations will also continue to grow in the field of digital employee experience.

10.3 One more crucial question...

Back to the question in the introduction to this chapter. So, you can opt for the blue pill and go along with the digital illusion. Perhaps we will achieve total enlightenment in the digital workplace of tomorrow.

Or you can choose the red pill and wake up from your virtual dream, to live and work with others, sometimes with all the inconveniences that come with life, and to strive for a more *human workplace*.

Red or blue, which pill do you take?

11 Acknowledgements

This book would not exist without the most important people in our own lives. Thank you, Annette, Nathan, Micha, Kemo and Raimi for your encouragement and patience. Because writing and translating this book, there seemed to be no end to it. But it is there! So, we now have (a little) more time.

Our special thanks go to Robbert Jan Sabel for his substantive feedback on our text, with which we have really been able to give this book more depth. In addition, we would also like to thank Gerhard Minten for his critical reading, which has enabled us to fine-tune the consistency and structure of our book.

We would also like to thank James Robertson for his DEX body of thought, which we have regularly been able to draw on in recent years. We are pleased with his beautiful forward to this book and are happy to contribute to the worldwide DEX movement as 'pioneers'.

Finally, we would like to thank friends, family, clients, business partners and all those other people in our network — online and offline — for the various suggestions we received. For example, about the title and cover of our book. With that, it has not only become *our* book, but hopefully also a bit *your* book.

So, the 'credits' are over, but if you have made it all the way here, we would love to take you to our post-credits scene.

Do you take the blue pill or the red pill or...?
In the summer of 2018, Marleen Stikker, internet pioneer, member of the Dutch Advisory Council for Science, Technology and Innovation and director of Waag, Future Lab for technology and society in Amsterdam was a guest on 'Zomergasten'[28] (a Dutch TV series featuring in-depth interviews). During the interview she showed the famous red and blue pill excerpt from The Matrix and described the red pill as the urge to look under bonnet. But, according to Stikker once you start doing that, "you also see all kinds of things that you can no longer *not* see".

That is certainly our experience too. The promise that technology holds in organisations is great, but it often does not make the daily work of 'the employee' any easier. Sometimes it even makes us a bit sad, because we regularly see the problems coming from miles away.

Stikker does not want to choose between a blue or red pill, but advocates a third pill (a pink one): with that third pill, or third way "you do not necessarily just fight the evil you encounter, but you also work on what you consider desirable and

---

[28] https://www.vpro.nl/programmas/zomergasten/kijk/afleveringen/2018/marleen-stikker.html#c8c94218-ecfc-4e18-ad83-781a50cd0bfd

possible". According to her, you can also pursue "a possible reality".

In the interview Stikker also mentioned the example of The Digital City, the first Dutch free access portal and virtual community on the internet, which she founded in 1993: "It didn't exist yet, but I could imagine it. So, you can work on something you can imagine, and as you work on it, you are realising it".

We also do not believe that the choice is only blue or red. We regularly dream of ultramarine blue vistas. At the same time, we move into the daily scarlet-red reality, where employees work *and* struggle with technology in their organisations.

We see this as a nice mix, but we would like to opt for the purple pill. Purple is a reddish-blue or bluish-red colour whose boundaries are not clearly defined. The colour purple is seen as a symbol of passion, inventiveness, inspiration, originality, spirituality, and hope, but is also the colour of sadness and mourning.

For us, the purple pill symbolises the search for the optimal mix for your organisation, your department or team and also for yourself: your own digital employee experience. It can take on many shades — from deep indigo to pale mauve and from dark orchid to soft lavender — because tastes, organisations and people differ.

12 About the authors

Tabhita Minten

Tabhita works as management consultant, with focus on digital and social innovation. In 2013, Tabhita started her own consultancy PeperMint.

As a strategic advisor, methodology expert, change agent, process director, facilitator, and scrum coach she works on improving student, employee, and customer experience.

Tabhita combines more than twenty years of experience as an organisational and communication consultant with knowledge of HR, information management and IT, and thus connects diverse groups, teams, and departments in organisations. With her clear long-term vision and pragmatic approach, she gets people moving.

Previously, Tabhita worked as project manager and product owner for a large number of intranet projects, as web manager at the Province of Utrecht, as an (online) consultant and communication advisor at various agencies and as a district manager at the municipality of Deventer.

You can read more about Tabhita on pepermint.nl.

Christiaan Lustig

Christiaan is a digital employee experience and digital workplace strategist. He helps organisations to continuously improve their internal digital communications, services, and collaboration.

Christiaan combines his extensive experience in (online) communication with his knowledge of digital tools and platforms, and of digital work and collaboration.

Christiaan is an independent consultant working mainly in the Netherlands and Belgium. He was founder of consultancy Brayton House, which he sold to TrueLime, and previously worked at Entopic and Sabel Communicatie.

Christiaan regularly speaks at digital workplace and other conferences in his native Netherlands, but also in Belgium, Germany, Denmark, Finland, Italy, Australia, and the United States.

You can read more about Christiaan on christiaanlustig.nl.